# WAR OF
# THE FLEA

ALSO BY ROBERT TABER

*M-26: Biography of a Revolution*

# WAR OF THE FLEA

## THE CLASSIC STUDY OF GUERRILLA WARFARE

### ROBERT TABER

#### With a Foreword by Bard E. O'Neill

BRASSEY'S, INC.
Washington, D.C.

**Library of Congress Cataloging-in-Publication Data**

Taber, Robert.
    War of the flea : the classic study of guerrilla warfare / Robert Taber ;
with a foreword by Brad E. O'Neill.— 1st [Brassey's] ed.
        p.   cm.
    Originally published: New York : L. Stuart, 1965.
    Includes index.
    ISBN 1-57488-555-3 (alk. paper)
    1. Guerrilla warfare.   I. Title.
    U240 .T1523   2002
    355.02'18—dc21                                                      2002074447

Printed in the United States of America on acid-free paper that meets the American National Standards Institute Z39-48 Standard.

Brassey's, Inc.
22841 Quicksilver Drive
Dulles, Virginia 20166

First Edition

10   9   8   7   6   5   4   3   2   1

*In Memory Of An*
*Old Fashioned American*
GEORGE A. THURSTON

# FOREWORD

When *The War of the Flea* first appeared in the late 1960s, revolutionary warfare waged by guerrilla forces representing the poor and deprived sectors of society was very much in vogue in radical political circles around the world. From the jungles of Indochina to the open spaces of Palestine, left-wing intellectuals believed that at last the poor had found a way to bring the rich and powerful to their knees and usher in a new egalitarian political era. The main inspiration and impetus was provided by the thinking of Mao Tse-tung, who had conceptualized and successfully carried out a protracted popular war based on well-organized, mass, popular support and guerrilla warfare, largely in rural areas.

Mao's success was emulated successfully by the Viet Minh against the French in the late 1940s and early 1950s. Little more than a decade later the Viet Cong, also following a Maoist blueprint, were poised to reap the fruits of victory against the South Vietnamese and Americans. Together with past revolutionary victories in Cyprus and Palestine and more recent ones in Algeria and Cuba, these events solidified the confidence and momentum associated with the strategy of protracted popular war that many came to believe would usher in a new progressive era.

Robert Taber was clearly swept up by these events and the romanticism surrounding them. While some of his predictions about the future may have been exaggerated and unsustainable, Taber's descriptive analysis of the nature of protracted popular war and what accounted for its victories was on the mark and endures to this day. This is the principal value of his work in the early 21st Century.

Not surprisingly, many things have changed since Taber's book first appeared. Two of these are particularly noteworthy.

First, and most important, our analytical concepts have broad-ened and become far more precise. Second, the process of glob-alization has significantly transformed the social, economic, and political makeup of the global environment. Both must be con-sidered if we are to place Taber's book in a context that makes it useful and relevant, if not compelling.

As far as analytical concepts are concerned, scholars and prac-titioners have disentangled and defined terms like insurgency, revolutionary warfare, guerrilla warfare, and terrorism, which in earlier and less discriminating times were often used inter-changeably. Insurgency—or internal war—is now viewed as a general overarching concept that refers to a conflict between a government and an out group or opponent in which the latter uses both political resources and violence to change, reformu-late, or uphold the legitimacy of one or more of four key aspects of politics. Those aspects are (1) the integrity of the borders and composition of the nation state, (2) the political system, (3) the authorities in power, and (4) the policies that determine who gets what in the society. The question is which ones are relevant in a particular case. The answers will vary greatly. Some insur-gents, like the Tamil Tigers in Sri Lanka and the Polisario in Western Sahara, seek to separate from an existing nation state to create their own. Others, like the Revolutionary Armed Forces of Colombia (FARC) or the Armed Islamic Group in Algeria, focus on replacing the political system and authorities with ones more to their liking. In what may seem counterintuitive, other insurgents, like the Ulster Defense Association in Northern Ire-land, fight to sustain or preserve the four aspects of politics, es-pecially the political system.

The ultimate goals or end states desired by insurgents also vary significantly and may include creating new independent countries, egalitarian social-political orders, theocracies based on religious laws, pluralist democracies, or a more equitable dis-tribution of wealth within an existing system. Alternatively, they may, as suggested, include keeping things the way they are. The last one alone makes it clear that not all insurgencies are "revo-lutionary." And, among those that are, there may be very differ-ent ultimate goals. Clearly, this wider conceptualization of insurgency goes well beyond that of the late 1960s when all insurgents were considered revolutionary egalitarians that wanted to fundamentally alter the society and polity.

Distinguishing terrorism from guerrilla warfare has further sharpened the analysis of insurgency. While there may be some minor differences in phraseology, most analysts define terrorism as the threat or use of physical coercion against non-combatants to create fear in order to achieve political objectives. Guerrilla warfare, by contrast, consists of hit-and-run attacks against police and military and the physical infrastructure that supports them. Insurgents may opt for one or both forms of warfare and, in some cases, might even choose to carry out conventional attacks with regular troop formations.

Insurgents also vary when it comes to the strategies they adopt. Not all prefer the protracted popular war strategy that is the centerpiece of Taber's work. Indeed, some prefer a military focus strategy that gives less prominence to political organizing and mass support, while still others opt for either a small-scale conspiratorial approach or urban warfare. How faithfully they follow their strategy and fulfill its requirements is another matter, as Taber illustrates in his discerning assessment of the failure of the communist insurgents in Greece during the late 1940s.

It may fairly be asked where *The War of the Flea* fits within this expanded analytical frame of reference. To put it another way, what is its utility today? I think there are two positive answers here. First, the category of insurgencies that Taber discussed in a clear, concise, informed, and at times passionate manner (especially in chapters 3–9) are still with us: witness the previously mentioned FARC and the New People's Army in the Philippines. Moreover, it is quite possible that the growing inequalities within and among states that are a by-product of the ongoing process of globalization will spawn new insurgents who espouse the strategy of protracted popular war and all it entails. Should that come to pass, we will have to revisit and understand the dynamics, assumptions, successes, and failures associated with that strategy. This is exactly the point where Taber's insights will be invaluable.

Five considerations discussed by Taber are especially important. The first is how an awareness of deprivations and a belief that they can be rectified through armed struggle creates and maintains the "will to revolt." Second is the disciplined strategic mindset that seeks to avoid enemy strength while attacking enemy weaknesses through countless attacks by dispersed guerrilla units. A third is the metamorphosis of the protracted armed struggle from the strategic defensive, to the strategic stalemate, to the strategic offensive. Fourth is the crucial role that political organization and base areas play in energizing and sustaining the struggle. Fifth, and no doubt most important, is how the government responds to the insurgent challenge, since governments have an incredible knack for being their own worst enemies because of their proclivity to overreact with indiscriminate violence against innocent people.

Taber's discussion of these important factors can also shed light on contemporary conflicts that have a very different ideological complexion from the insurgent movements of his era. Consider, for example, the resounding defeat of the Israelis in southern Lebanon by Hezbollah guerrillas in the 1990s, or what the longer term future holds for Israel in its conflict with the Palestinians over its occupation of large parts of the West Bank and isolated settlements in Gaza Strip. Indeed, a familiar theme that transcends the decades and is redolent of many passages in Taber's commentary can be seen in the following words of Ze'ev Sternhell in Israel's most prestigious newspaper, *Ha'aretz*, on April 5, 2002:

> As far back as 10 years ago, the General Headquarters of the Israel Defense Forces warned the government that there is no military solution to the uprising in the territories. Indeed, there are light years separating the mentality of those people and the frightening oversimplification evinced daily by the present government and chief of staff. All the primitive methods of using force and more force against a popular uprising have already been tried by occupying armies in the last century. The result has always been the same: Guerrilla fighters who enjoy the support of the population can easily drag a regular army, heavy-handed and insensitive, into actions that arouse even more hatred. It has

always been the case that acts of oppression have only increased resistance.

In the end, the guerrilla wins a political victory because people that are fighting for their freedom always ultimately achieve their aim. Humiliated peoples arise from the ashes: Only a sick mind could hope that occupying the territories will bring an end to the guerrilla warfare and to terror. On the one hand, it is reasonable to suppose that terror will only increase and become more sophisticated and devastating, and on the other, a guerrilla war against the IDF, because of its massive deployment everywhere, will take on the dimensions of a general popular struggle and will earn international legitimization as a war of liberation.

The point here is obviously not to take sides in the Israeli-Palestinian dispute but rather to demonstrate that the kinds of ideas and propositions that Taber articulated are very much alive in our world and might profitably be used to analyze current conflicts and make informed judgements about their prospects.

Beyond specific situations, Taber's book can also provide a basis for stimulating a wide-ranging discussion of what has changed with respect to insurgency since the late 1960s. Here we may consider, among other things, what social, economic, and political developments dampened the ardor for revolution in many places Taber thought they would emerge, not the least of which were Latin America and the United States. We might also assess the opportunities and limitations of adopting a protracted popular war strategy for purposes very different from the Marxist egalitarian ones Taber wrote about. But, for such analysis to be intellectually productive, it must be grounded in the kind of succinct, knowledgeable, and explicit understanding of the phenomenon of protracted popular war that can be found in *The War of the Flea*.

Bard E. O'Neill
Washington, D.C.

# CONTENTS

## I

The wind of revolution. Popular will as the key to strategy.
The confrontation of the haves and the have-nots. Fallacies of
counterinsurgency. Guerrilla war as an extension of politics.
Cracks in the armor of the modern state.

## II

The war of the flea. Political and military objectives. Creating
"the climate of collapse." Organization of insurgent forces.
Guevara on guerrilla war: the base.

## III

Inception and evolution of an insurgency. Transition to civil
war. Alternative solutions. The Cuban example.

## IV

Protracted war. Popular forces versus regular armies. The
guerrilla as missionary. Mao Tse-tung on the war of the flea.
The lessons of China.

## V

Colonial war and the French experience. Strategy and tactics
of Vo Nguyen Giap. How the Vietminh won in Indochina.

## VI

## VII

## VIII

## IX

## X

## XI

# THE WIND OF REVOLUTION. POPULAR WILL AS THE KEY TO STRATEGY. THE CONFRONTATION OF THE HAVES AND THE HAVE-NOTS. FALLACIES OF COUNTERINSURGENCY. GUERRILLA WAR AS AN EXTENSION OF POLITICS. CRACKS IN THE ARMOR OF THE MODERN STATE.

Over the Communist-dominated district of Ben Cat rendezvoused the largest helicopter armada in the history of warfare—96 choppers carrying rockets, machine guns and 1,000 assault troops. Supported by 4,000 infantrymen, Rangers and counter-guerrilla squads, the attack force hoped to encircle an estimated 1,500 to 2,000 Viet Cong "main force" troops who two weeks earlier had mauled four government battalions in a carefully executed ambush.

The big airlift was the war's worst-kept secret. In Saigon, government information officers alerted photographers several days in advance. When the troops hit the Ben Cat touchdown, most of the Viet Cong had already slipped away.

—*Time*, August 21, 1964.

\* \* \*

Two South Vietnamese Ranger companies fanned out across the flat grassland and scrub jungle 25 miles north of Saigon. On a routine mission to relieve an outpost attacked by Communist Vietcong guerrillas, the 200 men moved cautiously. They paused in a grove of rubber trees, then emerged into a field and headed toward a cluster of huts 400 yards away.

Suddenly, from all sides, the fierce rattle and clatter of

1

gunfire erupted. Men crumpled before they heard the noise. Others scattered. Lieutenant William Richter, their wiry American adviser, dived to the soggy ground. Looking up, he saw Vietcong regulars in green fatigues advancing for the kill. Richter leaped to his feet and ran for cover. But other Vietcong riflemen, crouched at the fringe of the field, caught him in a murderous cross fire.

Bullets slammed into his thigh. He fell, crawled into the sheltering underbrush, and somehow kept going. For six hours, helped by survivors, he dragged himself back to Binh My, his home base. He was lucky; on the field beyond the rubber trees, 51 Rangers lay dead.

"They just lured us through a trap-door, closed it on our behinds, and let us have it," Richter later explained it. "We were caught flat-footed and cut to pieces."

"The same damn story," a senior U.S. officer in Saigon grumbled. Different only in detail or degree, similar stories unfold week after week in South Viet Nam. Posts are raided, officials assassinated, hamlets burned, towns assaulted. And they all add up to one gloomy conclusion: Despite inferior firepower and strength, the Communists are beating a South Vietnamese force of more than 400,000 soldiers backed up by 17,000 American advisers and nearly two million dollars a day in U.S. aid.

—Stanley Karnow, "This Is Our Enemy,"
*Saturday Evening Post*, August 22, 1964.

This is guerrilla war: the *guerra de guerrillas* fought by Spanish partisans against Napoleon's invading army, refined in our time to a politico-military quasi-science—part Marxist-Leninist social theory, part tactical innovation—that is changing the power relationships of the post–World War II era, and in the process is destroying the verities of the Western general staffs whose professional concern it is, and increasingly will be, to understand and to combat it.

Guerrilla war has become the political phenomenon of the mid-twentieth century, the visible wind of revolution, stirring hope and fear on three continents. At this writing it is being waged in a score of countries, from Angola to Iraq and from the Congolese bush to the suburban slums of Caracas. As the American commitment in Viet Nam deepens, it has become the first concern of the Pentagon, the Central Intelligence Agency, the National Security Council, the White House. It is being fought in a desperate, often silent struggle in our own Hemisphere, in Guatemala, Venezuela, Colombia. And it threatens, or *almost* threatens, to break out in the United States itself. Certainly it influences the thinking of Negro militants from Harlem to the Deep South: Gasoline bombs bursting in city streets not long ago gave tangible evidence of that influence.

In the world at large, it is destroying the vast vestiges of feudalism and of traditional colonialism where these remain. Its full vigor is turned now against neo-colonialism and against what, in Marxist terminology, is called imperialism—the economic and political (and often military) domination of the weak, industrially poor nations by the rich, powerful, and technologically superior ones.

Within the technologically backward areas, it is liberating the masses of the poor from the oppression of the privileged landowning and mercantile classes, from the oligarchies and the military juntas. And in the process—so it is charged and so it may happen—it is delivering them to another sort of tyranny, that of the authoritarian socialist state.

Viewed from one standpoint, it is a potent weapon, a sword of national liberation and social justice; viewed from another, it is a subversive and sinister process, a sort of plague of dragon's teeth, sown in confusion, nourished in the soil of social dissension, economic disruption, and political chaos, causing armed fanatics to spring up where peaceful peasants toiled.

In its total effect, it is creating new alignments and a new confrontation of powers that vitally relates to and yet transcends the Cold War. It is a confrontation, in its essence, of the world's *haves* and the world's *have-nots*, of the rich nations and the poor nations.

It is reshaping the world that we have known, and its outcome may well decide the form and substance of the foreseeable future, not only in the present theatres of war, which are vast and shadowy, but everywhere.

The questions then arise: What is it? What can be done about it—or with it? How to end it or to exploit it? Is it something that can be turned off and on at will, as an instrument of national policy or political expedience?

On the available evidence, most of it concentrated in a span of twenty years or so of what may be called the post-colonial period, a definition offers itself that will, in turn, suggest answers to other questions.

Guerrilla war, in the larger sense in which we have been discussing it, is *revolutionary war*, engaging a civilian population, or a significant part of such a population, against the military forces of established or usurpative governmental authority.

The circumstances may vary. In one instance—Israel and Algeria serve as examples—the authority may be alien, that is, colonial, and its opposition virtually the entire native population, led by a vanguard of militants.

In another set of circumstances—South Viet Nam or Cuba, for example—the authority may be a native, at least nominally independent government, and the insurgency initiated by a small political faction, challenging the policies, ideology, or legitimacy of the regime.

Again the cases vary. The war of the Viet Cong is ideological, with a strong class basis, and at the same time is powerfully nationalistic. Although led by Communists, it appeals not only to those who see it as a war against poverty and exploitation, but also those who are repelled by the corruption of the ruling hierarchy. It attracts those who will no longer tolerate military dictatorship, and the multitude of Vietnamese nationalists (*patriots* is the term we would use if speaking of ourselves in a similar situation) who consider the conflict a continuation of the long colonial struggle against the French, today replaced by foreigners of another stripe—the Americans who support and direct a succession of Vietnamese military juntas in the name of liberty and democracy.

Where the war in South Viet Nam has ideological and nationalistic roots, the revolution in Cuba had none that were visible. It began, rather, as the idealistic protest of a tiny faction of uncertain political orientation—vaguely "liberal," vaguely socialistic, tinged with Spanish anarchism—against the corruption and oppression of a police state. Class rivalries were not evident. Nationalism was not an apparent factor. The clash with foreign and feudal interests, the anti-Americanism, the militant proletarianism and Marxist slogans of the Cuban revolution were later developments, following rather than leading to the overthrow of Batista.

In Morocco (1952–1956), the nationalists of the Istiqlal built their cause around the symbolic figure of the exiled sultan, Mohammed Sidi ben Youssef, and forced the abdication of the pretender and the dissolution of the French protectorate. In Israel, powerful religious and ethnic drives gave the struggle for the Jewish national homeland the character of a holy war. In much of Africa (Congo, Cameroons, Angola), tribal rivalries and ambitions appear to play as great a part as does anticolonialism.

Nationalism, social justice, race, religion—beneath all of these symbolic and abstract "causes" that are rallying cries of the revolutions of the past two decades, one discovers a unifying principle, a common mainspring.

It is a revolutionary *impulse,* an upsurge of popular *will,* that really has very little to do with questions of national or ethnic identity, or self-determination, or forms of government, or social justice, the familiar shibboleths of political insurgency. It is not even certain that economic deprivation in itself is the decisive factor that it is widely assumed to be. Poverty and oppression are, after all, conditions of life on the planet that have been endured by countless generations with scarcely a murmur.

The *will to revolt,* so widespread as to be almost universal today, seems to be something more than a reaction to political circumstances or material conditions. What it seems to express is a newly awakened consciousness, not of "causes" but of *potentiality.* It is a spreading awareness of the possibilities of human existence, coupled with a growing sense of the *causal* nature of the universe, that together inspire, first in individuals, then in communities and entire nations, *an entirely new attitude toward life.*

The effect of this sudden awareness, this sudden fruition of consciousness, is to produce in the so-called backward areas of the world, all at once, a pervasive and urgent desire for radical change, based on the new insight, startling in its simplicity, that the conditions of life that had seemed immutable *can*, after all, be changed.

Limitations that were formerly accepted all at once become intolerable. The hint of imminent change suggests opportunities that had not been glimpsed until now. The *will to act* is born. It is as though people everywhere were saying: *Look, here is something we can do, or have, or be, simply by acting. Then what have we been waiting for? Let us act!*

This, at any rate, describes the state of mind of the modern insurgent, the guerrilla fighter, whatever his slogans or his cause; and his secret weapon, above and beyond any question of strategy or tactics or techniques of irregular warfare, is nothing more than *the ability to inspire this state of mind in others*. The defeat of the military enemy, the overthrow of the government, are secondary tasks, in the sense that they come later. The primary effort of the guerrilla is to militate the population, without whose consent no government can stand for a day.

The guerrilla is subversive of the existing order in that he is the disseminator of revolutionary ideas; his actions lend force to his doctrine and show the way to radical change. Yet it would be an error to consider him as a being apart from the seed bed of revolution. He himself is created by the political climate in which revolution becomes possible, and is himself as much an expression as he is a catalyst of the popular will toward such change.

To understand this much is to avoid two great pitfalls, two serious areas of confusion, into which counterinsurgency specialists seem to fall.

One such pitfall is the *conspiracy theory:* the view that revolution is the (usually deformed) offspring of a process of artificial insemination, and that the guerrilla nucleus (the fertilizing agent, so to speak) is made up of outsiders, conspirators, political zombies—in other words, actual or spiritual aliens—who somehow stand separate from their social environment, while manipulating it to obscure and sinister ends.

The other is the *methods fallacy,* held—at least until very recently—by most American military men: the old-fashioned notion that guerrilla warfare is largely a matter of tactics and techniques, to be adopted by almost anyone who may have need of them, in almost any irregular warfare situation.

The first view is both naive and cynical. Invariably expressed in the rhetoric of Western liberalism and urging political democracy (that is to say, multiparty elections) as the *desideratum*, it nevertheless lacks confidence in popular decisions; it tacitly assumes that people in the mass are simpletons, too ignorant, unsophisticated, and passive to think for themselves or to have either the will or the capacity to wage a revolutionary war.

*Ergo*, the revolution which in fact exists must be due to the machinations of interlopers. The guerrillas must be the dupes or the wily agents of an *alien* power or, at least, of an *alien* political philosophy.*

On the more naive level, it seems to be assumed that people would scarcely choose the revolutionary path of their own accord; certainly not if the revolution in question were out of joint with the political traditions and ideals held dear by Americans. To quote former President Eisenhower in this connection, relative to the war in South Viet Nam:

*"We must inform these people (the South Vietnamese) of what is happening and how important it is to them to get on our side. Then they will want to choose victory."*†

Alas! the victory they seem to have chosen is not General Eisenhower's.

Most American foreign policymakers and experts of the new politico-military science of counterinsurgency (the theory and practice of counterrevolution) appear more cynical than General Eisenhower. It is manifest in their pronouncements that all mod-

---

*But what can this strange American word, "alien," mean to the Vietnamese, to the Cubans, to the Congolese? Could it mean—shocking thought!—*American?*

†In a Republican political forum in Philadelphia, urging an "intensive propaganda campaign" to create a clear "unity of view between the South Vietnamese people and the United States"; quoted in *The New York Times*, June 16, 1964.

ern revolutions are, or are likely to become, struggles between two world "systems," the Communist on one side, the Americans and their allies on the other, with the people most directly involved merely pawns, to be manipulated by one side or the other.

Since it is the United States that is, more often than not in this era, the interloper in almost any revolutionary situation that comes to mind (Viet Nam, Cuba, Iran, Guatemala, Brazil, Congo, Venezuela, to name a few), it is not surprising that the Cold War psychology should lead us to look for our Russian or Chinese counterpart in the given area of contention, and, finding him, or thinking so, to assign to him a major role. To do so, however, is to succumb to a curious illogic, in which our powers of observation seem to fail us.

The following excerpt from an article entitled "Plea for 'Realism' in Southeast Asia" by Roger Hilsman, former United States Assistant Secretary of State for Far Eastern Affairs, is fairly typical:

> Any analysis of the situation in South Vietnam [writes Hilsman] should probably start with the realization that we are *not* dealing with a war. The problem is more political than military, involving acts of terrorism rather than battles. Out of a population of 14 million, the Communist Vietcong numbers only 28,000 to 34,000 regular guerrilla troops plus 60,000 to 80,000 part-time auxiliaries. *Its campaign is more like the gangland warfare of the nineteen thirties and the teenage terrorism of New York today than the war in Korea or World War II. In a very real sense, the F.B.I. has had more experience in dealing with this kind of problem than the armed services.*

Hilsman's article appeared in *The New York Times Magazine*, August 23, 1964.

The italics are added, perhaps unnecessarily. Putting aside the patent absurdity of his comparisons—"teenage terrorism" indeed!—Hilsman's analysis suffers from grave defects of observations and interpretation.

Out of a population that is closer to sixteen million than to fourteen million, the Viet Cong did not have *only* twenty-eight thousand guerrillas, etc. It had *as many as* twenty-eight thousand, and President Johnson's decision early in 1965 to expand the war by the punitive bombing of military targets in North Viet Nam made it amply clear how potent a force that was.

By way of comparison, Fidel Castro's Cuban guerillas, fighting on an island with a population of close to seven million, *never at any time exceeded fifteen hundred armed men.* Yet when the decisive battle of Santa Clara came in December of 1958, cutting the island in two, the whole city, except for the isolated military garrison, became involved in the conflict. And when Batista finally fled the country on the last day of the year, virtually the entire population of Cuba claimed participation in the victory. Far from being isolated or indifferent, all had been rebels, it seemed.

With respect to the question of popular support of the Viet Cong in South Viet Nam, Hilsman himself admits: ". . . *the vast majority of the Vietcong are recruited in the South; their food and clothing are procured in the South, and they collect 'taxes' in the South to import other supplies through Cambodia.*"

On this same question, Walter Lippman wrote in the *New York Herald Tribune* in April, 1964: "*The truth, which is being obscured for the American people, is that the Saigon government has the allegiance of probably no more than 30 per cent of the people and controls (even in daylight) not much more than a quarter of the* [national] *territory.*"

It should be fairly obvious that when a Vietnamese army of four hundred thousand men, supported by two divisions of American military "advisers," an immense armada of fighter planes, jet bombers, and helicopters, and financial infusions on the order of close to *two million dollars a day,* cannot control an insurgency, something more than "teenage terrorism" is involved. The error that the Viet Cong insurgency is the work of a fanatical minority directed from outside the country nevertheless persists, fostered by Washington for reasons which will be examined in subsequent chapters.

Can guerrilla tactics be employed successfully against guerrillas? The answer is negative. To suppose otherwise is to fall into the *methods fallacy*. Indian fighters do not become Indians by taking scalps. A spotted jungle suit does not make a United States marine a guerrilla.

The experience of World War II and of every conflict since then has made it clear that commando troops are not guerrillas. Nor can the so-called "counterinsurgency" forces now being developed in a more sophisticated school be considered guerrillas, although they may employ some of the more obvious techniques of the guerrilla fighter—the night raid, the ambush, the roving patrol far from a military base, and so on.

Such techniques are as old as warfare itself. It is possible to conceive of their use by Cro-Magnon man, whoever *he* was, against the last of the Neanderthals; they were employed by the aboriginal Britons against Caesar's legionnaires, and they are the techniques of savages in the Columbian jungle and no doubt of a few surviving New Guinean headhunters to this day.

Headhunters are not guerrillas. The distinction is simple enough. When we speak of the guerrilla fighter, we are speaking of the *political partisan*, an armed civilian whose principal weapon is not his rifle or his machete, but his relationship to the community, the nation, in and for which he fights.

Insurgency, or guerrilla war, is the agency of radical social or political change; it is the face and the right arm of revolution. Counterinsurgency is a form of counterrevolution, the process by which revolution is resisted. The two are opposite sides of the coin, and it will not do to confuse them or their agents, despite superficial similarities.

Because of the political nature of the struggle, the disparity of the means at the disposal of the two forces, and, above all, the total opposition of their strategic aims, the most fundamental tactics of the guerrilla simply are not available to the army that opposes him, and are available only in the most limited way to the counterinsurgency specialist, the United States Special Forces officer, let us say, who may try to imitate him.

The reasons are clear.

First, the guerrilla has the initiative; it is he who begins the war, and he who decides when and where to strike. His military opponent must wait, and while waiting, he must be on guard *everywhere*.

Both before and after the war has begun, the government army is in a *defensive* position, by reason of its role as policeman, which is to say, as the guardian of public and private property.

The military has extensive holdings to protect: cities, towns, villages, agricultural lands, communications, commerce, and usually some sort of industrial base to defend. There is also the purely military investment to consider: garrisons, outposts, supply lines, convoys, airfields, the troops themselves and their valuable weapons, which it will be the first tactical objective of the guerrillas to capture, so as to arm more guerrillas. Finally, there is a political system, already under severe strain if the point of open insurrection has been reached, to be preserved and strengthened.

In all of these areas, the incumbent regime and its military arm present highly vulnerable targets to an enemy who is himself as elusive and insubstantial as the wind.

For, while the army suffers from an embarrassment of wealth, and especially of expensive military hardware for which there is no employment, the guerrilla has the freedom of his poverty. He owns nothing but his rifle and the shirt on his back, has nothing to defend but his existence. He holds no territory, has no expensive and cumbersome military establishment to maintain, no tanks to risk in battle, no garrisons subject to siege, no transport vulnerable to air attack nor aircraft of his own to be shot down, no massed divisions to be bombarded, no motor columns to be ambushed, no bases or depots that he cannot abandon within the hour.

He can afford to run when he cannot stand and fight with good assurance of winning, and to disperse and hide when it is not safe to move. In the extremity, he can always sink back into the peaceful population—that sea, to use Mao Tse-tung's well worn metaphor, in which the guerrilla swims like a fish.

The population, as should be clear by now, is the key to the entire struggle. Indeed, although Western analysts seem to dislike entertaining this idea, it is the population which is doing the struggling. The guerrilla, who is of the people in a way which the government soldier cannot be (for if the regime were not alienated from the people, whence the revolution?), fights with the support of the noncombatant civilian populace: It is his camouflage, his quartermaster, his recruiting office, his communications network, and his efficient, all-seeing intelligence service.

Without the consent and active aid of the people, the guerrilla would be merely a bandit, and could not long survive. If, on the other hand, the counterinsurgent could claim this same support, the guerrilla would not exist, because there would be no war, no revolution. The cause would have evaporated, the popular impulse toward radical change—cause or no cause—would be dead.

Here again we come to the vital question of *aims*, on which the strategy and tactics of both sides are necessarily based.

The guerrilla fighter is primarily a propagandist, an agitator, a disseminator of the revolutionary idea, who uses the struggle itself—the actual physical conflict—as an instrument of agitation. His primary goal is to raise the level of revolutionary anticipation, and then of popular participation, to the crisis point at which the revolution becomes general throughout the country and the people in their masses carry out the final task—the destruction of the existing order and (often but not always) of the army that defends it.

By contrast, the purpose the counterrevolutionary is negative and defensive. It is to restore order, to protect property, to preserve existing forms and interests by force of arms, *where persuasion has already failed*. His means may be political insofar as they involve the use of still more persuasion—the promise of social and economic reforms, bribes of a more localized sort, counterpropaganda of various kinds. But primarily the counterinsurgent's task must be *to destroy the revolution by destroying its promise*—that means by proving, militarily, that it cannot and will not succeed.

To do so will require the total defeat of the revolutionary vanguard and its piecemeal destruction wherever it exists. The alternatives will be to abdicate the military effort in favor of a political solution—for example, the partition of Viet Nam after the French defeat at Dien Bien Phu, the Algerian solution, etc.; in other words, compromise or complete surrender.

That military victory against true guerrillas is possible seems doubtful on the basis of modern experience, barring the use of methods approaching genocide, as applied notably by the Germans in certain occupied countries during World War II.

The counterinsurgent cannot win by imitating the insurgent, because he is the alien in the revolutionary situation, and because his tasks are precisely the opposite of those of the guerrilla, where symmetry exists at all. The guerrilla's mere survival is a political victory: it encourages and raises the popular opposition to the incumbent regime. Thus he can afford to run and to hide. The counterinsurgent gains nothing by running and hiding. He surrenders everything. The guerrilla can disguise himself as—in fact he can be—a peaceful agrarian worker, and still spread his revolutionary message. In a similar role, the counterinsurgent would be merely a police spy, and would accomplish little, spread no message. The guerrilla can hit and run. Every successful raid gives him more arms and ammunition, and more favorable publicity. The counterinsurgent can gain nothing by such Red Indian tactics—even if similar targets were available to him—and they are not. His military campaign must be sweeping, continuous, and cumulative in its effects. Either he clears the country of guerrillas, or he does not. If he does not, he continues to lose.

The distinction made here between guerrilla war as a politico-military technique and mere guerrilla-ism (banditry on the one hand or the application of irregular warfare techniques by regular military organizations on the other) is by no means as arbitrary as it may at first appear.

Popular insurrections have occurred throughout history. They have usually failed, or in any case have produced only limited victories, because the techniques they can exploit today were then irrelevant to the historical situation. This is simply another way of saying that, until now, the popular majorities, the laboring, unspecialized masses of pre-industrial societies, were able to exert very little political or economic leverage.

The serfs of the medieval period, for example, were unable to resist the feudal military power not merely because they lacked arms and skills, political consciousness, and cohesion, but because they had no other means to affect the political and economic processes of their world.

Economically, they were manageable because they lived too close to the level of bare subsistence to be otherwise. They could not even think of withholding their labor—their only economic lever. Isolated by their brute condition and their ignorance, they lived below the level of politics. If they starved, or rebelled and were slaughtered, *there was no one to care,* no economically or politically potent class to whom it would make the slightest difference.

Subsequent revolutions, from the Renaissance to the Russian revolution and not excluding Mexico, 1910–1917, have been bourgeois in character, or have quickly been converted into bourgeois movements, after an initially populist period. *"Liberté, égalité, fraternité"* applied only to the great and petite bourgeoisie of France, after a brief Jacobin interval (significantly, all bourgeois historians loathe and fear the proletarianism of the Terror), because, in the end, only the bourgeoisie had the lever—wealth and the tools of production—to assume leadership in a confrontation with the landowning feudal aristocracy. Although there was now some class mobility and a greater need of democratic slogans, the landless, unspecialized masses remained submerged. They could remain idle and starve. All the better. It reduced beggary and banditry. Isolated, they could be slaughtered and *no one would care.*

History brings us to a pass in which (for a variety of reasons but principally because of the complexity of the productive processes, the fragmentation, specialization, and interlocking nature of the industrial society, and the importance of disciplined labor and huge consumer markets, relative to the profit system) the laboring masses assume political potency. Their new role in the industrial society—as producer, as distributor, as consumer—gives them a lever. If they withhold their work, the economy collapses. If they cease to buy and to consume, the same thing happens. If they are slaughtered, there are worldwide repercussions, based, in the final analysis, on economic considerations.

The modern industrial society cannot function, and its government cannot govern, except with popular participation and by popular consent. What is true of the industrial state is also true, with minor qualification, of the nonindustrial states and colonies on which the former depend for the raw materials of their industry and, often, for their export markets.

For the best of economic reasons, modern governments must seem to be popular. They must make great concessions to popular notions of what is democratic and just, or be replaced by regimes that will do so. The governments of the dominant industrial states themselves, even more than those they dominate, are strapped politically by this factor of the domestic "image." They must use the liberal rhetoric and also pay something in the way of social compromise—schools, hospitals, decent concern for the well-being of all but the most isolated poor—if they are to retain power and keep the people to their accustomed, profit-producing tasks.

This fact makes such governments extremely vulnerable to a sort of war—guerrilla war with its psychological and economic weapons—that their predecessors could have ignored, had such a war been possible at all in the past.

They are vulnerable because they must, at all cost, keep the economy functioning and showing a profit or providing the materials and markets on which another, dominant economy depends. Again, they are vulnerable because they must maintain the appearance of normalcy; they can be *embarrassed* out of office. And they are triply vulnerable because they cannot be as ruthless as the situation demands. They cannot openly crush the opposition that embarrasses and harasses them. They must be wooers as well as doers.

These are modern weaknesses. They invite a distinctly modern development to exploit them, and that development is modern guerrilla warfare. The weaknesses peculiar to the modern, bourgeois-democratic, capitalistic state (but shared in some measure by all modern states) make popular was possible, and give it its distinctive forms, which clearly cannot be imitated, except in the most superficial way, by the armies of the state itself.

Fundamentally, the guerrilla's tactics and those of the counterinsurgent differ because their roles differ. They are dissimilar forces, fighting dissimilar wars, for disparate objectives. The counterinsurgent seeks a military solution: to wipe out the guerrillas. He is hampered by a political and economic inpediment: he cannot wipe out the populace, or any significant sector of it. The guerrilla, for his part, wishes to wear down his military opponent and will employ suitable tactics to that end, but his primary objective is political. It is to feed and fan the fires of revolution by his struggle, to raise the entire population against the regime, to discredit it, isolate it, wreck its credit, undermine its economy, overextend its resources, and cause its disintegration.

Essentially, then, the guerrilla fighter's war is political and social, his means are at least as political as they are military, his purpose is almost entirely so. Thus we may paraphrase Clausewitz: *Guerrilla war is the extension of politics by means of armed conflict*. At a certain point in its development it becomes revolution itself—the dragon's teeth sprung to maturity.

Guerrilla war = revolutionary war: the extension of politics by means of armed conflict.

Until this much is properly understood by those who would oppose it, nothing else about it can be understood and no strategy or tactics devised to suppress it can prevail.

If, on the other hand, this much is understood by those who lead it, then it can scarcely fail in any circumstance—for the war will not even begin until all the conditions of its success are present.

Let us now begin to examine the mechanics of the revolutionary process called guerrilla warfare.

## THE WAR OF THE FLEA. POLITICAL AND MILITARY OBJECTIVES. CREATING "THE CLIMATE OF COLLAPSE." ORGANIZATION OF INSURGENT FORCES. GUEVARA ON GUERRILLA WAR: THE BASE.

*The enemy advances, we retreat; the enemy camps, we harass;*
*the enemy tires, we attack; the enemy retreats, we pursue.*
*—Selected Military Writings of Mao Tse-tung*

What Mao Tse-tung says of guerrilla tactics here is a key to Communist thinking; it can be discerned in diplomacy as well as in war. The Soviet policymakers have mastered the Chinese lesson very well, and apply it to a wide variety of problems having nothing to do with guerrilla fighting. Berlin since World War II has been a prime example, and the establishment of Soviet missile bases in Cuba was another.

But then, why not? The policy of hitting the enemy when he is weak, evading him when he is strong, taking the offensive when he falls back, circling around when he advances—all of this is only common sense. There is no great novelty in it, nor can the Marxist-Leninist camp claim any especial credit for it.

What *is* new—and Mao is the apostle and the long Chinese revolution the first proving ground—is the application of guerrilla activity, in a conscious and deliberate way, to specific political objectives, without immediate reference to the outcome of battles as such, provided only that the revolutionaries survive.

Oddly enough, however, it is the non-Communist Cubans rather than the Chinese who have provided the most clear-cut

**17**

example of military activity producing political effects, in a war in which few of the battles would be described by military men as more than skirmishes, yet one in which the government came crashing down as surely as if an army had been destroyed on the battlefield.

The explanation seems to baffle military men, yet it is simple enough; Guerrillas who know their trade and have popular support cannot be eliminated by the means available to most governments. And on the other hand, few governments can stand the political, psychological, and economic stresses of guerrilla war, no matter how strong they may be militarily.

In general, all warfare involves the same basic problem: how to use one's strength to exploit the enemy's weaknesses and so to overcome him. In an internal war, the government's strength is its powerful army, its arsenal, and its wealth of material means. Its weaknesses are social, political, and economic in the sense that the economy, while an asset, is vulnerable from several points of view. It provides both military and psychological targets.

Constitutional democracies, as I have already noted, are particularly exposed to the subversion that is the basic weapon of revolutionary war. The stratified class structure and the multiparty political systems of most such countries are sources of political and social dissension that can be exploited. Constitutional law is a further embarrassment, and sometimes may be a fatal impediment.

Fulgencio Batista fell, not because he was a dictator, but because his situation in a country with democratic institutions— moreover, a country almost entirely dependent on the favor of the United States with its similar institutions and traditions— did not permit him to be dictator *enough* to resolve the contradictions that confronted him. His hands were tied by conventions he could not break without losing his foreign support. His use of counterterrorism, that is, the *illegal* use of force, only increased his domestic opposition. Yet without it, he had no effective means to combat the disorder and subversion that threatened his regime. Similarly, the French in Indochina were destroyed, in the final analysis, by the very ideas and institutions that they themselves had introduced. Franco, by way of contrast, probably stands because he has successfully stifled the very idea of political liberty in Spain, while putting enough bread on the table to satisfy the vocal majority.

This is to speak of legalistic—that is, social and political—difficulties.

On the military level, a regular army, under whatever political system, has disadvantages that are owing to the very size and complexity of the organization, and again to its defensive role, as the guardian of the national wealth and of the whole of the national territory.

The guerrilla, for his part, finds his strength in his freedom from territorial commitments, his mobility, and his relationship to a discontented people, as the spokesman of their grievances, the armed vanguard, as Che Guevara puts it, of militant social protest.

His weakness is merely—I use the word advisedly—a *military* weakness. He lacks the arms, and usually the manpower, to risk a military decision.

In the circumstances, it is obvious what the guerrilla's tactics must be.

Politically, he must seek to aggravate such social and political dissension as exists and to raise the level of political consciousness and of revolutionary *will* among the people. It will also be part of his design, as well as the natural consequence of his actions, to bring about an intensification of the political repression that already exists, so deepening popular opposition to the regime and hastening the process of its dissolution.

Militarily, his tactics will be designed to wear the enemy down, by chipping away at the morale of the government troops and by inducing the maximum expenditure of funds, material, and manpower in the effort to suppress him. At the same time he will endeavor to build his own forces through the capture of government arms and by recruitment from an increasingly alienated populace, avoiding a military confrontation until the day—and it will come late—when an equalization of forces has been obtained.

An army deals from strength, seeking out the enemy's weaknesses in order to destroy him. The guerrilla is sometimes said to deal from weakness, but this is an absurdity. In fact, he exploits his own kind of strength, which lies in the extreme mobility of lightly armed forces without territorial or hardware investments, a bottomless well of manpower from which to recruit, and the fact that *time*—which is both money and political capital—works in his favor.

Analogically, the guerrilla fights the war of the flea, and his military enemy suffers the dog's disadvantages: too much to defend; too small, ubiquitous, and agile an enemy to come to grips with. If the war continues long enough—this is the theory—the dog succumbs to exhaustion and anemia without ever having found anything on which to close his jaws or to rake with his claws.

But this may be to oversimplify for the sake of an analogy. In practice, the dog does not die of anemia. He merely becomes too weakened—in military terms, overextended; in political terms, too unpopular; in economic terms, too expensive—to defend himself. At this point, the flea, having multiplied to a veritable plague of fleas through long series of small victories, each drawing its drop of blood, each claiming the reward of a few more captured weapons to arm yet a few more partisans, concentrates his forces for a decisive series of powerful blows.

Time works for the guerrilla both in the field—where it costs the enemy a daily fortune to pursue him—and in the politico-economic arena.

Almost all modern governments are highly conscious of what journalism calls "world opinion." For sound reasons, mostly of an economic nature, they cannot afford to be condemned in the United Nations, they do not like to be visited by Human Rights Commissions or Freedom of the Press Committees; their need of foreign investment, foreign loans, foreign markets, satisfactory trade relationships, and so on, requires that they be members in more or less good standing of a larger community of interests. Often, too, they are members of military alliances. Consequently, they must maintain some appearance of stability, in order to assure the other members of the community or of the alliance that contracts will continue to be honored, that treaties will be upheld, that loans will be repaid with interest, that investments will continue to produce profits and be safe.

Protracted internal war threatens all of this, for no investor will wish to put his money where it is not safe and certain to produce a profit, no bank lends without guarantees, no ally wishes to treat with a government that is on the point of eviction.

It follows that it must be the business of the guerrilla, and of his clandestine political organization in the cities, to destroy the stable image of the government, and so to deny it credits, to dry up its sources of revenue, and to create dissension within the frightened owning classes, within the government bureaucracy (whose payrolls will be pinched), and within the military itself.

The outbreak of the insurgency is the first step—it is a body blow that in itself inflicts severe damage on the prestige of the regime. The survival of the guerrilla force over a period of time, demonstrating the impotence of the army, continues the process. As the guerrilla's support widens—and this will come automatically as the weakness of the government is revealed—political trouble is sure to follow, in the form of petitions, demonstrations, strikes. These in their turn will be followed by more serious developments—sabotage, terror, spreading insurrection.

In such circumstances, it will be a remarkable government that will not be driven to stern repressive measures—curfews, the suspension of civil liberties, a ban on popular assembly, illegal acts that can only deepen the popular opposition, creating a vicious circle of rebellion and repression until the economy is undermined, the social fabric torn beyond redemption, and the regime tottering on the verge of collapse.

In the end, it will be a question whether the government falls before the military is destroyed in the field, or whether the destruction of the military brings about the final deposition of the political regime. The two processes are complementary. Social and political dissolution bleeds the military, and the protracted and futile campaign in the field contributes to the process of social and political dissolution, creating what I have elsewhere called "the climate of collapse."

This is the grand strategic objective of the guerrilla: to create

the "climate of collapse." It may be taken as the key to everything he does.

*     *     *

Please note, I do not by any means wish to suggest that the
train of events described above can be put into motion anywhere, at any time, by any agency, irrespective of objective and
subjective conditions. Insurrections may be provoked or incited
or may occur spontaneously as the expression of grievances or
of frustrated aspirations or because of other factors: religious
frenzy, blood feuds; mass hysteria induced by anything from a
sports contest to a rape in Mississippi can lead to bloodshed
and temporary anarchy. Guerrilla warfare does not necessarily
follow. Insurrection is a phenomenon, revolution a process,
which cannot begin until the historical stage has been set for it.

Since guerrilla war is, in our definition, a revolutionary process, it can only come out of a revolutionary situation. For this
reason, I am inclined to agree with Che Guevara when he writes
in *Guerrilla Warfare:*

> Naturally, it is not to be thought that all conditions for revolu-
> tion are going to be created through the impulse given to them
> by guerrilla activity. It must always be kept in mind that there
> is a necessary minimum without which the establishment and
> consolidation of the first center [of rebellion] is not practicable.
> People must see clearly the futility of maintaining a fight for so-
> cial goals within the framework of civil debate. When the forces
> of oppression come to maintain themselves in power against es-
> tablished law, peace is considered already broken.
>
> In these conditions, popular discontent manifests itself in more
> active forms. An attitude of resistance crystallizes in an outbreak
> of fighting, provoked initially by the conduct of the authorities.
>
> Where a government has come into power through some form
> of popular vote, fraudulent or not, and maintains at least an ap-
> pearance of constitutional legality, the guerrilla outbreak cannot
> be promoted, since the possibilities of peaceful struggle have not
> yet been exhausted.

We have defined guerrilla war as the extension of politics by
means of armed conflict. It follows that the extension cannot
logically come until all acceptable peaceful solutions—appeals,

legislative and judicial action, and the resources of the ballot box—have been proved worthless. Were it otherwise, there would be no hope of enlisting the popular support essential to revolutionary activity.

If people are to accept the risks and responsibilities of organized violence, they must believe first that there is no alternative; second, that the cause is compelling; third, that they have reasonable expectation of success. The last named is perhaps the most powerful of motives.

Where the cause appears just, the situation is intolerable, and oppression past all appeal, the way to action is clear.

Even then, however, much groundwork must be done before a guerrilla campaign will become feasible.

The experiences of Algeria, of Cuba, and of other successful revolutions indicate that, in most circumstances, guerrillas require the active support of a political organization outside of their own ranks but dedicated to their cause, an urban arm of the revolutionary movement that can provide assistance by means both legal and illicit, from placing bombs to defending accused revolutionaries in the courts of law (assuming that these still exist).

Isolation, military and political, is the great enemy of guerrilla movements. It is the task of the urban organization to prevent this isolation, to provide diversions and provocations when needed, to maintain contact, to keep the world aware of a revolution in progress even when there is no progress to report.

Usually the revolutionary political organization will have two branches: one subterranean and illegal, the other visible and quasi-legitimate.

On the one hand, there will be the activists—saboteurs, terrorists, arms runners, fabricators of explosive devices, operators of a clandestine press, distributors of political pamphlets, and couriers to carry messages from one guerrilla sector to another, using the towns as communications centers.

On the other hand, there will be sympathizers and fellow travelers, those not really *of* the underground, operating for the most part within the law, but sustaining the efforts of the activists, and, of themselves, accomplishing far more important tasks.

The visible organization will, of course, have invisible links with the revolutionary underground, and, through it, with the guerrillas in the countryside. But its real work will be to serve as a respectable facade for the revolution, a civilian front, or, as the Cubans called it, *resistencia civica*, made up of intellectuals, tradesmen, clerks, students, professionals, and the like—above all, of women—capable of promoting funds, circulating petitions, organizing boycotts, raising popular demonstrations, informing friendly journalists, spreading rumors, and in every way conceivable waging a massive propaganda campaign aimed at two objectives: the strengthening and brightening of the rebel "image," and the discrediting of the regime.

# INCEPTION AND EVOLUTION OF AN INSURGENCY. TRANSITION TO CIVIL WAR. ALTERNATIVE SOLUTIONS. THE CUBAN EXAMPLE.

Let us say that a cause exists. Peaceful alternatives have been exhausted. The revolutionary organizations have come into being, perhaps only in skeletal form, but sufficient to the immediate need.

Somewhere in the remotest province, which will be the most revolutionary because the most neglected and the most favorable to guerrilla action because the most primitive and inaccessible, insurrection breaks and spreads.

A rebel band springs into existence, composed of armed civilians who call themselves patriots, and whom the government will call bandits or Communists.

A government arsenal is assaulted, a police post is burned, a radio station is briefly seized, and a proclamation is issued in the name of the revolution. The hour is at hand, the people are in arms, the tyrant (or puppet, or foreigner) must go. A blow has been struck for national liberation and the lines of battle are drawn.

The aims and principles of the revolution are specified in appropriate rhetoric, with patriotic references and historical footnotes. They are just aims, worthy principles. Who would propound any others? They involve popular grievances, and they strike a popular response.

The towns and the countryside are abuzz with rumors. Young men and boys who have longed for the day of decision hasten to consult one another as to the role that each can, or should, or will play in the conflict to come. Members of the opposition parties, who have heretofore confined their intransigence to the lecture platform and the writing of editorials, now must take a position. The blow that has been struck is a catalyst, deciding new alignments and future attitudes. Who will join the rebels? Who will walk the neutral line, or abandon his principles and make common cause with the oppressor?

Since it is not in the nature of governments to treat with armed civilians, the insurrection must be put down, order established, and confidence restored. Already there are discreet questions being put by foreign embassies, and although these embassies want reassurance, they are not above consulting with the political opposition; they may even establish an informal liaison with the rebels, both to gain intelligence and by way of insurance. Business leaders and banks, both foreign and domestic, will be close behind, and not always so discreet. The situation, if allowed to develop, is certain to attract foreign journalists, and the rebels, perhaps insignificant in themselves from the government's point of view, will then find the platform from which to amplify their cause—and the embarrassment of the regime—a thousandfold.

The government is not concerned about the loss of a few policemen, or even an arsenal, but it *is* terrified of the attendant publicity, which casts doubts on its stability and thus on the future of the economy. Besides, who knows what other insurrections may not be brewing?

Reassuring statements are issued, provincial garrisons are quietly reinforced. An expedition is sent, with as little fanfare as possible, to extirpate the bandits, root and branch.

Now is the critical time for the revolution. If the insurrection has been well timed, the terrain well chosen, and the guerrilla leaders competent and determined, the military effort will fail. The experience of scores of guerrilla campaigns in the era since World War II—indeed, of the American Revolution and of the Peninsular War in Spain (1804–14)—shows that it is virtually impossible to stamp out guerrillas in rural areas where they have room to maneuver and to hide, assuming that they also have the support of the rural population. Conceivably it may be accomplished by exterminating the rural population itself, but such draconian methods failed even the Nazis in eastern Europe, and not for scruples or lack of determination on their part.

This is not to say that guerrillas can win battles. In the early stage of the insurgency they will have no business to seek battles and every reason to shun them. Rather, the rebel strategy will be:

(1) To attack only when assured of success by the overwhelming superiority of firepower, position, and the element of surprise, and only in pursuit of limited objectives, such as the capture of arms, or to create a diversion from some other action, or to avoid encirclement;

(2) To use the campaign as an educational tool and a propaganda weapon by disclosing the impotence of the enemy, showing that he can be defied with impunity; to proselytize among the rural population by identifying with its grievances and aspirations and by putting the burden and the blame of bloodshed on the repressive government as the clear aggressor it will necessarily become in the course of the anti-guerrilla campaign.

In the beginning, only small actions in isolated sectors will be possible. Later, as the guerrillas grow stronger, they will divide their forces, to take their revolutionary message into new areas, and to harass the army on a broader scale, forcing it to extend its lines so that its defenses are weakened, and small units can be reduced, one at a time.

Throughout the campaign to the final stage, the rebel strategy will be to avoid a military decision, until an equalization of forces has been reached, and the government army can be confronted on the battlefield with clear assurance of success.

At the onset, defiance will be enough. The existence of insurgency will in itself serve to discredit the government and so to advance the rebel cause. The difficulty will be to continue to make political capital of an uprising that can consist, initially, of only small actions. Just as the regime depends for its life on an appearance of stability and progress, so does the rebel leader depend on action as the means of asserting his intransigence and winning mass support.

*   *   *

The guerrillas have struck their opening blow. The moment hot pursuit dies, they must turn and strike again—at the vanguard of the expeditionary force or its outposts, at a supply column, at a depot where arms can be obtained.

If their clandestine organization in the towns is up to it, there will now be incidents of terrorism or of industrial sabotage, to heighten the crisis. If there are atrocities in the way of reprisal on the part of the authorities, they must be well publicized. If there are martyrs, there must be big funerals, protests led by the mothers of the slain, outcries of popular indignation. Ideally there will be a general strike. With it will come further repression, a curfew, beatings, arrests, creating further alienation of the populace from the regime, perhaps creating new martyrs, new incidents.

As it becomes clear that the government can no longer maintain order and cannot suppress the insurrection, the revolutionary tide begins to rise and swell. Students join the ranks of the underground. The working class and liberal middle-class elements of the towns—housewives, white-collar workers, the "out" political factions, the economic nationalists, idealists of one sort or another, and the disaffected of all classes—join the popular protest against persecution and the loss of civil liberties. Hunted members of the clandestine organization flee to the countryside to join the guerrillas, and peasants who have become the victims of a military compaign which is sure to claim innocent casualties, or who have fallen under suspicion for their association with the rebels, also swell the insurgent force.

As it grows, it becomes capable of action over wider territory; even more important, it becomes capable of establishing guerrilla bases in areas which the military can no longer control. With the establishment of such bases come into being a rebel government and a guerrilla economy, capable of supporting the guerrilla fighters independently of raids and smuggled supplies from the towns.

In a later phase, the base areas are expanded, continual pressure being maintained against the government forces on their perimeters, until the guerrillas hold or operate freely in most of the rural territory of entire regions, confining the army, except for excursions which will grow shorter and more dangerous as time passes, to their fortified strong points in the towns.

At this point, the conflict begins to resemble a civil war between territorial entities of the same nation, each of its separate economy and government. There will, however, be significant differences: (1) The territory of the guerrillas will be rural and its economy agricultural and primitive, while the economy of the enemy will be industrial—continuing to present targets for sabotage—and his territory increasingly restricted to urban areas; (2) the legitimate government will continue to suffer all the pangs and pressures, political, diplomatic, economic, of a regime confronted by open insurgency which it cannot suppress, while the rebels will only gain prestige and popular appeal by their successful insurgency.

\*     \*     \*

We have been discussing characteristic developments in a revolutionary situation, from the start of an insurgency to the point at which a relative balance of forces is reached. The question remains as to *what sort* of decision will follow—military or political.

In the smaller, semi-colonial countries with economies and to some extent governments dependent on richer and more powerful neighbors (Cuba is the revolutionary prototype), I am inclined to believe that the political decision, the easier and less costly of the alternatives, is almost always possible—barring outside intervention.

The Cuban revolution provides an excellent example of the process that we have been discussing in hypothesis.

The stage had been set much as I have decided it above.

In December of 1956, Fidel Castro and eighty-one armed followers disembarked from a leaking motor cruiser on the lonely shore of Cuba's easternmost province of Oriente, arriving from Mexico. In the month that followed, the force was reduced to a round dozen, most of the other men being killed or captured in a military ambush before they could make their way into the mountains.

Castro's military activities during the next six months were minuscule. They consisted of small raids on isolated army posts (yet the first produced sufficient captured weapons to double the force, when recruits were found), sugar mills, and villages on the edge of the Sierra Maestra range. When I first met Castro in the Sierra in April of 1957, he had perhaps one hundred followers. Half of these had arrived only two weeks before from Santiago, the provincial capital, where they had formed the bulk of his urban underground.

The biggest single action of the *fidelistas* during this period was an attack, May 28, 1957, on the small military outpost of Ubero, manned by about seventy soldiers. Rebel losses came to eight dead; military losses were put at thirty. Other actions during the first year were on a similar scale, or smaller, and at no time during the entire insurrectionary period did battles involve more than a few hundred men on either side. In almost all cases of unprovoked attack, where there was no prior move by the Batista military, the rebel purpose was to capture weapons with which to arm more guerrillas.

The scale of the action was miniature, yet propaganda victories came early and were international in their scope. One followed the other. The reports of *The New York Times* correspondent Herbert Matthews made Fidel Castro's name a household word in the United States; subsequent publicity carried it around the world.

The effect, on the political and economic level, was to bring about an American arms embargo against the government of Fulgencio Batista, to discourage investment and restrict credits to such an extent as to put a severe strain on the regime, and to cause, gradually, a failure of nerve within the administration that spread to the military and made it practically impotent long before most of the troops had ever heard a rifle shot.

The Batista regime was hopelessly corrupt and inefficient. When it fell, it appeared, superficially, to have fallen of its own weight and weakness. Foreign journalists covering the story could not quite believe that Castro's handful of bearded riflemen had had much to do with it, except on the propaganda level.

At first, Batista had been disdainful of what appeared to be a small band of political adventurers, almost completely isolated in the remote Sierra Maestra. After the first fitful attempts to flush the guerrillas out of the mountains, he was inclined to dismiss the danger, and to cede to Castro by default a territory so remote, inaccessible, thinly populated, and uneconomic as to be scarcely worth bothering about. Bandits had existed in the Sierra before; they had attracted little attention and had done no great harm. Doubtless Batista reasoned that the publicity would soon die away and that in due time the adventurers would be starved out of their sanctuary, or grow weary of a fruitless campaign and give it up.

Later he was to feel that he had grossly underestimated the threat, and to see rebels everywhere—even where there were none.

With a secure mountain base, Castro was able to recruit a strong irregular force, and to make what he had seem many times stronger than it actually was. Fast-moving guerrilla patrols, sometimes of only half a dozen men, managed to be everywhere at once. No army patrol was quite safe in the mountains; no outpost, sugar plantation, or village was safe in the foothills or within striking distance of them.

When Castro grandiosely announced a "total war" in March of 1958 and warned of "columns" moving quickly north, east, and west toward key objectives in all parts of the island, the army reacted as to an invasion. It had no way of knowing that the "columns" consisted of fewer than two hundred men in all, or that a so-called "second front," announced at the same time, had been opened in northern Oriente by a force of no more than sixty-five guerrillas—their heaviest weapon a .30-caliber Browning automatic rifle.

At the onset of the insurrection, Batista had sent five thousand soldiers to the Sierra Maestra to cordon off the area and eliminate the guerrillas.

The Sierra runs more than one hundred miles east and west and is fifteen to twenty-five miles deep. Simple arithmetic shows how impossible was the task set for the army, given a trackless terrain of precipitous and thickly wooded mountains. It would have been impossible with twice the number of troops.

Aircraft were used against the guerrillas, but as Castro noted, the thick, wet woods blotted out the effects of high explosive bombs and napalm within twenty-five to fifty yards. These was little danger even had the bombardiers been accurate and the location of the guerrillas known—and neither of these "ifs" ever prevailed. The only damage done by the aircraft was to the thatched *bohios* of the mountain dwellers, living in cultivated clearings.

The Sierra quickly became the first *territorio libre* of the revolution, and the first year was devoted by the free-ranging guerrillas to building a rear-base economy—small shops for the fabrication of uniforms and equipment, for making crude explosive devices and for repairing arms, for canning foodstuffs, and so on—and proselytizing the inhabitants of the zone.

The harassment of the outlying districts and the interception of army patrols were undertaken as a matter of course. It was relatively easy because of the superior military intelligence of the guerrillas—thanks to the cooperation of the *guajiros*. Seldom was a military patrol able to come within even a few miles of the *fidelista* force without the guerrillas becoming aware of it.

One of Castro's first acts on entering the Sierra had been to execute two bandits, accused of rape and murder, so dramatically establishing a revolutionary government with a code of law, which could be looked to as a stabilizing force in an area long neglected by the Havana government.

The next step, important in winning a following politically and recruiting militarily, was to promulgate an agrarian reform law that conferred title on hundreds of small tenants, sharecroppers, and squatters, who were told that they now owned the land they tilled.

Similar tactics were followed in the more densely populated, rich coffee-growing uplands of the so-called *Segundo Frente, Frank Pais,* opened by Raul Castro. A code of law was imposed, taxes were collected, and certain benefits—schools, hospitals—were conferred in return. Supplies were scrupulously paid for—in cash. The villagers were treated much as they would have been treated by any ordinary government—except that political indoctrination was more intense and more was demanded of them, in the way of identification with the revolution and adherence to its goals.

The few rural guard posts in the area were quickly eliminated. Since they consisted of no more than a few men at each post, they presented no obstacle for even so small an "army" as that of Raul Castro, with sixty-five men, all of whom could be concentrated on a single objective at a time.

Army columns sent into the area were ambushed as they entered, and then, after brief resistance, allowed to pass. As they returned, they were likely to be ambushed again at other points—and again permitted to pass.

If pursued, the guerrillas simply withdrew into the wooded hills, dispersed, and regrouped elsewhere. When the zone was clear, they returned to the villages. After a few weeks of this futile exercise, the army ceased to send patrols, and contented itself with strengthening the garrisons in the towns on the outskirts of the free territory. But as the rebel force grew from internal recruitment and its economy prospered, these garrisons, too, became unsafe, and had to be reduced in number for reasons of security.

In terms both of expense and of military manpower, it became simply uneconomical for the government to attempt to hold dozens of tiny villages and farms and to police an area several thousand square miles in extent; and so the military excursions ceased and the villages were abandoned to the rebels, the military having the larger towns and the uneasy provincial capital to defend. In this manner, the liberated territory was gradually extended. At its expanding periphery, a no-man's-land was created, visited by both rebels and Batista troops but held by neither. Slowly, bits of this neutral strip were also nibbled away, as not worth fighting for, and the free zone continued to grow.

Within three months, the army found itself unable to protect the big American nickel and cobalt mines on Oriente's northern coast, except in daylight. For reasons of political expedience, these were permitted to continue in operation. But the rebels helped themselves to such motor transport as they were able to use—several dozen jeeps and trucks from the mines—and earth-moving equipment for building new roads and improving those that existed.

A rebel guard post was actually established within a few yards of the entrance to the great United States naval base at Guantanamo Bay. When the Americans were found to be fueling Batista's military aircraft on one occasion and supplying the air force with rockets on another—this after an arms embargo had been declared by the United States—Raul Castro's guerrillas promptly kidnapped fifty-odd American sailors and marines on an outing, along with their excursion bus, and simultaneously swooped down on the mining communities and a United Fruit Company experimental station to seize half a dozen executives and engineers as hostages.

The resultant embarrassment to Batista was great. It effectively demonstrated, to a world largely unaware of the dimensions of the guerrilla campaign in remote Oriente, that the dictator no longer had control of a considerable part of his country.

That the great United States itself could be defied by a few hundred Cuban guerrillas was a further political lesson—and a powerful one. It naturally increased pressure on Batista to "do something." In the circumstances, it is hard to see what he could have done. Short of exterminating his own people and burning their villages, he was helpless. In the extremity of the final months, a few military commanders in the field, subsequently executed as war criminals, began to wage such a scorched earth campaign. But by then it was far too late.

* * *

The rebels had built a strong force and a viable economy in secure rear-base areas. In northern Oriente, they had control of the entire national coffee crop, worth some sixty million dollars; since the government had to have it and could not get it in any other way, it was allowed to come to market, and was duly taxed by the guerrillas.

Other farm produce was also marketed. In addition to the

revenue it brought, it provided the guerrillas, in exchange, with supplies which they were unable to obtain within the liberated territory. The government needed the crops for the sake of its own economy; it was also in the position of having to maintain an appearance of normality, a pretense of business-as-usual (venality also played a part), and for these reasons tolerated a commerce that nourished the rebellion.

Guerrilla action continued, slow, sporadic, and small-scale, often serving merely as a distraction while the rebel build-up within the free zones continued, yet always having definite objectives: the gradual extension of the *territorio libre*, the capture of arms, the training of new recruits.

A similar process had been going on in the middle of the island, in the mountains of the Escambray in Las Villas Province, on a smaller scale. In the late summer of 1958, two columns from the Sierra Maestra, having taken part in the defeat and capture of a regiment-sized expedition sent into the mountains in June, left the Sierra to join the rebels in the Escambray, arriving in early September.

The campaign gradually intensified on both fronts. Guerrilla patrols began to interdict the main roads and the national highway, railroad bridges were destroyed, traffic in the country was brought to a virtual standstill, except for the movement of large military convoys; then these, too, began to come under fire.

What had been a few small bands of guerrillas became a swarm. Sabotage and terrorism were stepped up in the towns. On occasion, rebel jeep patrols drove boldly into cities to reconnoitre the suburban areas. Small towns along the national highway were isolated and their garrisons reduced. Santiago was cut off. In mid-island, an armored train carrying troops to defend the city of Santa Clara was derailed and set afire, and its military passengers captured, along with a huge supply of arms, enough to supply all of the young volunteers in the city.

The demoralized Batista soldiers, restricted first to the towns and then to their own fortified barracks, found no military profit in venturing out; since the guerrillas would not stand and fight, unless assured of overwhelming odds. On the other hand, the troops risked ambush and capture or death whenever they traveled in less than company or even battalion strength. Slowly, lacking unified leadership, their communications destroyed, they allowed themselves to be sequestered. When the hour of decision came, most of them were on guard within their own isolated fortresses, controlling not even the towns they were supposed to defend.

The army general staff and the government, meanwhile, had been shattered by a general crisis of nerves, with no member of the establishment able to trust another and each preparing to sell out or get out at the first sign of the regime's collapse. The loss of confidence in Batista had proceeded to such an extent that the ambassador of the all-powerful United States, on whom the Cuban economy depended and whose puppet the government was for all practical purposes, was in the process of negotiating with the political opposition, seeking a conservative alternative to Batista, when the latter precipitately fled the country, along with his generals and the ranking members of his government.

*    *    *

To summarize the Cuban revolution in this way is to neglect the part played by the urban underground and the civic resistance movement—both of which contributed much, in the way of strikes, demonstrations, sabotage, and propaganda work, to undermine the morale of the government and to destroy the prestige without which it could no longer direct the economy nor continue to exist.

Yet in the final analysis, it was the guerrillas, waging a war of attrition, slowly nibbling away the rural areas, gradually expanding the free territories and building a military force with captured arms while strangling the army in its barracks, whose action was decisive.

Virtually all of the weapons to arm some fifteen hundred men, save a few hundred small arms smuggled in from the United States, were captured from Batista's troops, a few dozen or at most a hundred at a time. The fall of the Oriente capital of Santiago put tanks and artillery into the hands of the rebels. Further surrenders in Las Villas gave them the means to confront any remaining army regiments that might have been disposed to fight.

But by that time, Batista had already fled, a general strike had put Havana in insurgent hands, the principal garrison at Camp Columbia, outside the capital, had surrendered without firing a shot, the navy had rebelled, and the war was over.

## PROTRACTED WAR. POPULAR FORCES VERSUS REGULAR ARMIES. THE GUERRILLA AS MISSIONARY. MAO TSE-TUNG ON THE WAR OF THE FLEA. THE LESSONS OF CHINA.

Revolutionary wars are generally, of necessity, wars of long duration. The seeds of revolution are slow to germinate; the roots and tendrils spread out silently underground long before there is any sign of sprout or bud. Then suddenly one day, like new wheat springing up in a cultivated field, there is a blaze of color, an overnight growth: the rebels are there and everywhere.

It is customary to speak of guerrilla wars as wars of attrition. The phrase is not perfectly accurate. Guerrilla warfare is not so much abrasive as subversive. It is a growth that penetrates the crevices of a rotting structure and one day bursts it asunder.

Yet attrition does, after all, play a great part. In the political sphere, the government is subjected to a constant, wearing pressure that comes from the great expense and anxiety of the anti-guerrilla campaign and from the constant cry of the opposition, the banks, the business community: *When will it all end? What are you doing about it?*

Economic attrition has already been discussed. Sabotage is one aspect of it. The loss of credit and investment suffered by a country engaged in civil war is the other, far more important, aspect. No small nation, and few great ones, can stand the deprivation indefinitely. Yet the painful fact is that the guerrillas, for their part, *can* carry on indefinitely.

Having no vested interest, no political opposition within their own ranks, no economic problems other than those that can be solved by extending the war and capturing what they need, the insurgents have nothing to lose and everything to gain by continuing the struggle. And, on the other hand, they have nothing to gain and everything to lose by giving up. In fact, once the banner of rebellion has been raised and blood has been shed, it is no easy matter to give up. The rebels begin to fight for whatever reason: they continue because they must.

They fight, then, in order to survive. Given their inferiority of resources, they can survive only by avoiding direct confrontation with a superior enemy; that is, battle on the enemy's terms. Guerrilla strategy is dictated from the start by this consideration. The result—if the guerrillas are to be successful and to avoid extermination—is a *protracted* war. The conflict must continue until the movement has recruited and trained enough men, and come into possession of enough arms, to build a revolutionary army capable of defeating the regular army in open battle.

Failing this, it must continue until political developments resulting from the campaign have brought about the desired end: the rising of the masses of the people and the overthrow or abdication of the discredited government.

In Cuba, the Batista regime collapsed before the military confrontation had fully developed. The army, lacking leadership, its general staff gone, found no reason to continue the struggle, and surrendered. A general strike in Havana—in other words, a rising of the people—was sufficient to make it clear to the military that there would be no further purpose in fighting; Batista had fled and his designated heirs could not be forced on the rebellious country. Nothing but a revolutionary government would be accepted.

Cuba is a prototype. It is typical of the dependent, semi-colonial countries in which revolution can be attained without the bloody necessity of full-scale war. In such countries, it will be sufficient, barring intervention by the dominating colonial power, to create by guerrilla warfare the conditions in which a discredited government (discredited because it can no longer keep order and assure a profit to the country's proprietors) falls from lack of support, and the revolutionaries rush in to fill the political vacuum.

All of the Central American dependencies of the United States and most of the South American republics, economic and political satellites of the United States, are in the same category as Cuba. Their governments can see the handwriting on the Cuban wall; so can Washington. Hence the almost hysterical efforts of the past six years to isolate Cuba, to keep the infection from spreading. If it does spread, and there is evidence that this has already happened to some extent, they may be expected to go the way of Cuba. However, to say so is to assume that the United States will *not* intervene militarily. Intervention would create an entirely new picture; one could expect to see Indochina re-created in Latin America. And revolutionary short-cuts, *à la Cuba*, would be out.

The remaining colonies of the European powers are in another category. Here, too, a political solution can obviate the necessity of a military showdown. Yet in the case of the actual colonies, it will not be a matter of discrediting the colonial power or its government, but simply of taking the profit and prestige out of colonialism. Cyprus provides a good example of an insurgency that was successful simply because terror, sabotage, and constant disorder made the island too unprofitable and politically embarrassing for the British to remain. They got out, finally, not because they were forced out, but because there was no longer any compelling reason to remain (and there were many good reasons for withdrawing).

In a third category are those revolutionary wars that must be won, at last, on the battlefield. China is the classic example, the laboratory in which principles were evolved that are still being proven today, in all the backward areas of the world.

Popular revolutionary forces *can* defeat regular armies. This is the fundamental lesson of China. Popular forces, to put the matter more precisely, can *become* armies, making the transition from guerrilla activity to mobile warfare, that will be superior on their own ground to regular troops equipped with all of the heavy weapons produced by modern industry.

How can a nation that is not industrialized defeat one that is? This, says former Deputy Assistant Secretary of State E. L.

Katzenbach, Jr., is the problem that confronted Mao Tse-tung.*
The answer, which applies to insurgency anywhere, as against
the mechanized army, is guerrilla warfare.

As Katzenbach sees it, Mao's approach to the theory of war as
applied to his own peculiar situation—that of China—was simply to shift the emphasis customarily given to the fundamental
components of previous military doctrine. Where the industrial
nations stressed such tangible military factors as arms, logistics,
and manpower, says Katzenbach, Mao looked to the *in*tangibles:
*time, space,* and *will.*

Lacking the arms with which to confront well-equipped armies in the field, Mao avoided battle by surrendering territory.
In so doing, Katzenbach writes, he traded *space* for *time,* and
used the time to produce *will:* the psychological capacity of the
Chinese people to resist defeat.

This is the essence of guerrilla warfare.

> Although Mao never stated it quite this way [writes Katzen-
> bach], the basic premise of his theory is that political mobilization
> may be substituted for industral mobilization with a successful
> military outcome. That is to say, his fundamental belief is that
> only those who will admit defeat can be defeated. So if the total-
> ity of a population can be made to resist surrender, this resistance
> can be turned into a war of attrition which will eventually and
> inevitably be victorious.

The context brings to mind the well-known quotation from
Mao: "With the common people of the whole country mobi-
lized, we shall create a vast sea of humanity and drown the
enemy in it."

As for the *time* factor, Katzenbach observes:

> Mao holds that military salvation stems from political conver-
> sion. But, note: Conversion takes time.

*E. L. Katzenbach, Jr., "Time, Space, and Will: The Politico-Military Views
of Mao Tse-tung," in *The Guerrilla—and How to Fight Him.* Edited by Col. T. N.
Greene; Frederick A. Praeger, Inc., Publishers.

So Mao's military problem was how to organize *space* so that it could be made to yield *time*. His political problem was how to organize *time* so that it could be made to yield *will*, that quality which makes willingness to sacrifice the order of the day, and the ability to bear suffering cheerfully the highest virtue. So Mao's real military problem was not that of getting the war over with, the question to which Western military thinkers have directed the greater part of their attention, but that of keeping it going.

Mao's problem, then: how to avoid a military decision. His answer: hit and run, fight and live to fight another day, give way before the determined advance of the enemy, and, like the sea, close in again as the enemy passes. The formula, *space* for *time*, is well conceived. But in his *Selected Military Writings*, Mao makes it clear that nothing is gained unless the time is used to produce political results, by raising the revolutionary consciousness, the *will* of the masses:

> When the Red Army fights, it fights not merely for the sake of fighting, but to agitate the masses, to organize them, and to help them establish revolutionary political power; apart from such objectives, fighting loses its meaning and the Red Army the reason for its existence.

Mao believes that revolutionary war itself is the university in which guerrilla fighters are schooled, and that war develops its own lessons and principles:

> Our chief method is to learn warfare through warfare. A person who has had no opportuntiy to go to school can learn warfare—he can learn through fighting in war. A revoluntary war is a mass undertaking; it is often not a matter of first learning and then doing, but of doing and then learning, for doing itself is learning. There is a gap between the ordinary civilian and the soldier, but it is no Great Wall, and it can be quickly closed, and the way to close it is to take part in revolution, in war.

Political mobilization—raising the level of political consciousness of the people and involving them actively in the revolutionary struggle—is the first task of the guerrillas; and it is the nature of this effort, which necessarily takes time, that accounts for the protracted character of revolutionary war. The study of Mao, however, discloses something more:

*Time is required, not alone for political mobilization, but to allow the inherent weaknesses of the enemy to develop under the stress of war.*

Mao makes this point more than once in his military writings, in several different contexts. In the Sino-Japanese war, for example, Japan, an industrial power, had the great advantage of a superior war machine, capable of striking devastating blows at the poorly armed troops of semi-feudal, semi-colonial, unindustrial China. Yet such an advantage, unless *immediately* decisive, could not compensate for defects that would become apparent in prolonged conflict.

The first of these was that Japan, while powerful militarily, lacked the base in natural resources and manpower to sustain her war machine, far from home and in a vast, populous country over a long period of time. Indeed, the war had been started to compensate for the defect, but extended through conquest Japan's paucity of material resources. Insofar as this was true, war was an act of desperation, and a contradiction, putting the cart before the horse. For, what would happen if the war was *not* won quickly and the new wealth quickly absorbed and exploited?

Japan was seeking, of necessity, a war of quick decision. The correct military response was to deny it, by avoiding a military confrontation and fighting along the lines of guerrilla and mobile warfare, trading the vast space of China for the time necessary (1) to let the inherent weaknesses of Japan develop and show themselves under the stresses of a protracted war; (2) to build Chinese resistance forces to the strength and degree of organization needed to confront the gradually weakened Japanese war machine.

As Mao analyzed the situation:

. . . Japan's war is conducted on the basis of her great military, economic and political-organizational power, but at the same time it rests on an inadequate natural endowment. Japan's military, economic and political-organizational power is great but quantitatively inadequate. Japan is a comparatively small country, deficient in manpower and in military, financial and material resources, and she cannot stand a prolonged war. Japan's rulers are endeavoring to resolve this difficulty through war, but again they will get the very reverse of what they desire; that is to say, the war they have launched to resolve this difficulty will end in adding to it and even in exhausting Japan's original resources.

Other defects were apparent:

... the internal and external contradictions of Japanese imperialism have driven it not only to embark on an adventurist war unparalleled in scale, but also to approach its final collapse. In terms of development, Japan is no longer a thriving country; the war will not lead to the prosperity sought by her ruling classes, but to the very reverse, the doom of Japanese imperialism. This is what we mean by the retrogressive nature of Japan's war. It is this reactionary quality, coupled with the military-feudal character of Japanese imperialism, that gives rise to the peculiar barbarity of Japan's war. All of which will arouse to the utmost the class antagonisms within Japan, the antagonism between the Japanese and the Chinese nations, and the antagonism between Japan and most other countries of the world.

... while Japan can get international support from the fascist countries, the international opposition she is bound to encounter will be greater than her international support. This opposition will gradually grow and eventually will not only cancel out support but even bear down on Japan herself. ... To sum up, Japan's advantage lies in her great capacity to wage war, and her disadvantages lie in the reactionary and barbarous nature of her war, in the inadequacy of her manpower and material resources, and in her meager international support.

Against the Japanese war-making capacity were pitted the Chinese advantages of space, time, and will. The long struggle for national liberation, as Mao notes, had tempered the Chinese people; social and political gains had created a *will* that was capable of great sacrifice and resistance over long periods of time; and:

Again by contrast with Japan, China is a very big country with vast territory, rich resources, a large population, and plenty of soldiers and is capable of sustaining a long war.

Space in which to maneuver, abundant manpower, strong international support, and the Chinese will to resist aggression—these were China's advantages. They were also the reasons for avoiding a quick decision in favor of a protracted war, one in which Japan's single advantage, superior arms and organization, would be worn away.

> . . . it can be seen that Japan has great military, economic, and political-organizational power, but that her war is reactionary and barbarous, her manpower and material resources are inadequate, and she is in an unfavorable position internationally. China, on the contrary, has less military, economic, and political-organizational power, but she is in her era of progress, her war is progressive and just, she is moreover a big country, a fact which enables her to sustain a protracted war, and she will be supported by most countries. The above are the basic, mutually contradictory characteristics of the Sino-Japanese War. They have determined and are determining the protracted character of the war and the fact that the final victory will go to China and not to Japan. The war is a contest between these characteristics. They will change in the course of the war, each according to its own nature; and from this everything else will follow.

Similar considerations determined the protracted character of the struggle against the warlords and later the Kuomintang during China's long civil war. In analyzing the Chinese situation, Mao notes the contradictions and conflicts of interest that arise on several planes: for example, between the various imperialist powers seeking dominance in China, within the Chinese ruling classes, and between the ruling classes on the one hand and the broad masses of the people on the other.

1. Conflict among the warlords and against the Nationalist government creates a heavier burden of taxation.

2. Heavier taxation cause the landlord class to exact more exorbitant rents from the peasants and increases the hatred of the latter for the landlords.

3. The backward condition of Chinese industry, as related to foreign industry and foreign concessions in China, causes a

more vicious exploitation of Chinese labor and drives the wedge deeper between the workers and the Chinese bourgeoisie.

4. "Because of the pressure of foreign goods, the exhaustion of the purchasing power of the workers and the peasant masses, and the increase in government taxation, more and more dealers in Chinese-made goods and independent producers are being driven to bankruptcy. Because the reactionary government, though short of provisions and funds, endlessly expands its armies and thus constantly expands the warfare, the masses of the soldiers are in a constant state of privation. Because of the growth in government taxation, the rise in rent and interest demanded by the landlord and the spread of the disasters of war, there are famine and banditry everywhere and the peasant masses and the urban poor can hardly keep alive. Because the schools have no money, many students fear that their education may be interrupted; because production is backward, many graduates have no hope of employment."

Mao's conclusion:

> Once we understand all these contradictions, we shall see in what a desperate situation, in what a chaotic state, China finds herself. We shall also see that the high tide of revolution against the imperialists, the warlords and the landlords is inevitable, and will come very soon. All China is littered with dry faggots which will soon be aflame. The saying, "A single spark can start a prairie fire" is an apt description of how the current situation will develop. We need only look at the strikes by the workers, the uprisings by the peasants, the mutinies of soldiers and the strikes of students which are developing to see that it cannot be long before a "spark" kindles "a prairie fire."

In his theory of guerrilla warfare, whether against domestic or foreign enemies, Mao distinguishes carefully the various phases of development of the campaign, laying particular emphasis on the first phase, which he calls the period of the *strategic defensive*.

In the beginning—and the first phase may last for many months—territory is nothing, attrition is everything. The enemy is permitted, even encouraged to expand where he will. The guerrillas give ground, conducting only harassing action, circling around, fighting always in the enemy's rear areas and presenting no continuous front for the foe to smash.

The enemy is engaged, during this period, in a strategic offensive, with the object of wiping out the guerrillas. On his part, the action is characterized by a series of "encirclement and suppression" campaigns (compare the so-called "clear and hold" efforts in South Viet Nam today, under American leadership) during which the effort is made to occupy territory and to rid it of guerrilla infestation, piecemeal.

The contradiction implicit in this effort is that it converts increasingly large parts of the national territory into government "rear areas" where guerrilla operations work best. The repressive forces succeed in encircling areas of guerrilla activity—no one stops them—but in the process they themselves become encirled by guerrillas, and while the guerrillas can almost always slip out of any given encirclement, by dispersion and exfiltration, how can the army slip out? Where is the front? It does not exist. Movements of men and material become progressively greater and more expensive; the lines of supply and communication become ever longer, more attenuated, and more vulnerable to guerrilla attack. In effect, the army, in occupying broad expanses of rural territory, abets the guerrillas by providing them with broader and easier targets and more accessible sources of arms and ammunition.

The guerrilla strategy remains constant during this period, although tactics vary with the situation. The strategy is to force the enemy to spread himself as thin as possible, by harassing him all along the line, wherever he is weak, and then to concentrate all available guerrilla strength to annihilate—never merely to rout—inferior enemy units, one at a time.

"Ours are guerrilla tactics," writes Mao. "They consist mainly of the following points:

¶ "Divide our forces to arouse the masses, concentrate our forces to deal with the enemy.

¶ "The enemy advances, we retreat; the enemy camps, we

harass; the enemy tires, we attack; the enemy retreats, we pursue.

¶ "To extend stable base areas, employ the policy of advancing in waves; when pursued by a powerful enemy, employ the policy of circling around.

¶ "Arouse the greatest numbers of the masses in the shortest time by the best possible methods.

"These tactics are just like casting a net; at any moment we should be able to cast it or draw it in. We cast it wide to win over the masses and draw it in to deal with the enemy."

In areas where little opposition is met, the net is cast. The guerrillas disperse, to carry on the work of political indoctrination, to strengthen the internal economy of the revolutionary movement, to establish rear base areas—bases which, it should be noted, can be expanded or contracted, or even abandoned, on short notice.

Where opposition is strong, the net is drawn in. The guerrillas are able to concentrate heavy forces—Mao recommends two, or four, or even six times the enemy strength—against a single enemy weak point.

Battles are not prolonged. On the contrary, it is Mao who has invented the "five-minute attack"; it consists of a sudden on-slaught, a brief and furious interval of fighting, and then the assault is broken off as suddenly as it began and the guerrillas rapidly retire, having inflicted as many casualties and taken as many arms as possible during the stated time but not lingering even a minute for more. Mao stresses the battle of quick deci-sion—the very opposite of Western military strategy. Where the army backed by heavy industry is able to make a long-drawn technological contest of each battle, relying on superiority of equipment and logistics to tell in the end, the guerrillas must rely on speed, superior position, and locally superior man-power, and must break off the engagement before the superior-ity of heavy weapons can take its toll.

As we have remarked before, the guerrilla fights the war of the flea. The flea bites, hops, and bites again, nimbly avoiding the foot that would crush him. He does not seek to kill his enemy at a blow, but to bleed him and feed on him, to plague and bedevil him, to keep him from resting and to destroy his nerve and his morale. All of this requires time. Still more time is required to breed more fleas. What starts as a local infestation must become an epidemic, as one by one the areas of resistance link up, like spreading ink spots on a blotter.

In the second phase of the campaign, the period of equilibrium, a stalemate sets in. The government finds it cannot destroy the guerrillas; for the moment it can only seek to contain them, while preparing new offensives for the future. The guerrillas cannot destroy the army: They continue to harass it, taking advantage of lulls in the conflict to expand the revolutionary base areas, nibbling away at the fringe of no-man's-land that surrounds each liberated zone, improving the internal economy of crops, workshops, arms repair depots, and using the time to agitate the people, to forward the war of propaganda, and to sharpen the internal conflicts that shake the enemy camp as the long, expensive anti-guerrilla campaign bogs down and the end appears hopelessly far away.

The third stage, that of the revolutionary strategic offensive, or general offensive, begins when the opposing forces of the government and those of the guerrillas have reached a balance, and the insurgents seize the military initiative, now no longer as pure guerrillas, but as mobile columns up to divisional strength, capable of confronting and destroying the army in open battle.

Where the insurgents formerly gave way at the approach of the enemy, or depended on hit-and-run ambushes, they will now give battle, using small units, to pin down the main forces of the government while their regular troops are thrown—always in superior numbers—into concentrated attacks on the most vulnerable objectives along the enemy's attenuated lines of support or weakest points of concentration.

When encircled, the rebels, instead of dispersing and exfiltrating under cover of darkness, as before, will concentrate and make a powerful breakthrough at a chosen point in the enemy's lines—again, perhaps using secondary troops to pin down the army in other areas.

Gradually, sometimes using guerrilla tactics, at other times concentrating for powerful strategic blows, the rebels will succeed in cutting the enemy's main lines of communication and isolating segments of the enemy's forces, which can be destroyed one at a time. The insurgents will themselves begin to hold territory, first expanding their rural bases until they have blotted up most of the countryside, making it untenable for the enemy, then seizing the villages and the larger towns, driving the army back into its urban strong points, which, once isolated, can be reduced piecemeal.

As the strong points are reduced and the army's manpower is whittled down, with big units captured or annihilated and others defecting (as may be expected if they are native troops), the rebels will come into possession of heavy weapons—tanks, artillery—which can be used to reduce even larger strong points, until at last a siege of the cities, aided by popular uprisings, brings the war to its successful termination in the destruction or surrender of the army and the collapse of the government.

\* \* \*

A principle can be observed throughout this entire process: the more the enemy holds, the more he has to defend and the broader the insurgent target area. Yet on the other hand, the more the insurgent fights and wins, the more he has with which to fight and to win—in arms, in manpower, in material resources. Thus the objectives of the government and of the insurgent must be diametrically opposed. The army seeks to end the war as quickly as possible, in order to minimize its losses; the insurgent seeks to prolong it, since he has everything to gain by it.

It is clear that the guerrilla objectives cannot be accomplished overnight, or even within any predictable period. It is a basic premise of Mao's theory that the phases of the campaign will overlap, that on many occasions setbacks will occur, mobile units may have to be dispersed, again to become guerrilla bands, the third phase may slip back into the second, territory that has been won may be surrendered, and may change hands many times before it can finally be consolidated as part of the spreading Red territory.

On a map, the areas of guerrilla activity will appear as tiny ink spots. Gradually they will become splotches, and the splotches will grow larger until they finally run together into solid red, spreading over the entire national territory. But note: The coloration will progress, not from east to west or north to south, but from the outside in, from the mountains and the jungles to the cultivated rural areas, then to the villages within those areas, then to the towns, and along the national highways, and only in the final struggle to the diminishing pin-pricks of the cities.

The principles of the operation may be observed in the Communist war on Chiang Kai-shek's Nationalist troops in the period immediately following World War II. Analyzing a campaign of seventeen months duration in 1946–47, during which 640,000 Nationalist troops were killed or wounded and 1,050,000 were captured, Mao lists the following points of insurgent strategy:

1. Attack dispersed, isolated enemy forces first; attack concentrated, strong forces later.

2. Take small and medium cities and extensive rural areas first; take big cities later.

3. Make wiping out the enemy's effective strength our main objective; do not make holding or seizing a city or place our main objective. Holding or seizing a city or place is the outcome of wiping out the enemy's effective strength, and often a city or place will be held or seized for good only after it has changed hands a number of times.

4. In every battle, concentrate an absolutely superior force (two, three, four, and sometimes even five or six times the enemy's strength), encircle the enemy forces completely, strive to wipe them out thoroughly, and do not let any escape from the net. In special circumstances, use the method of dealing the enemy crushing blows, that is, concentrate all-out strength to make a frontal attack and an attack on one or both of his flanks, with the aim of wiping out one part and routing another so that our army can swiftly move its troops to smash other enemy forces. Strive to avoid battles of attrition in which we lose more than we gain or break even. In this way, although inferior as a whole (in terms of numbers), we shall be absolutely superior in

every part and every specific campaign, and this ensures victory in the campaign. As time goes on we shall become superior as a whole and eventually wipe out all of the enemy.

5. Fight no battle unprepared, fight no battle you are not sure of winning; make every effort to be well prepared for each battle, make every effort to ensure victory in the given set of conditions as between the enemy and ourselves.

6. Give full play to our style of fighting—courage in battle, no fear of sacrifice, no fear or fatigue, and continuous fighting (that is, fighting successive battles in a short time without rest).

7. Strive to wipe out the enemy when he is on the move. At the same time, pay attention to the tactics of positional attack and capture enemy-fortified points and cities.

8. Replenish our strength with all the arms and most of the personnel captured from the enemy. Our army's main sources of manpower and material are at the front.

9. Make good use of the intervals between campaigns to rest, train, and consolidate our troops. Periods of rest, training, and consolidation should not be very long, and the enemy should so far as possible be permitted no breathing space.

Much of what Mao enumerates will seem obvious, but there are important points to note, some of which are in direct conflict with conventional military doctrine.

¶ Although the mobile warfare of insurgency resembles that of conventional forces, it is based on guerrilla strategy and works toward somewhat different objectives. The insurgents drive inward from rural areas toward the towns and then the cities. They occupy the hills and the woods before they seize the roads. In this, they behave in a manner diametrically opposite to the dictates of Western military strategy, in which strong points—industrial centers, communication centers, population centers—are hit first and the mop-up of the rural areas is left until last. What counts for the insurgents is not strong points, but territory that the enemy cannot contest without involving himself in a contradiction, that of extending his lines and weakening his effective striking force. Hence the rural areas first, the cities last.

¶ The main source of both rebel munitions and—in China—

rebel manpower is the opposing army. The Chinese armies were conscripted, badly paid or not paid at all, often ill-nourished and ill-clothed. The troops were themselves peasants; it was to be expected that defections would be common, and this was the case. Mao had no scruples, for that matter, about recruiting bandits; they were of the same class origin and in much the same condition as the Nationalist soldiers and those of the war lords, and could be easily indoctrinated to fight in the popular cause. His reasoning, no doubt, was that peasants who had some military training were easier to absorb than peasants who had had none. As to the question of supplies, it is a tenet of guerrilla theory, not only in China but in all revolutionary wars, that the enemy must be the main source of weapons and ammunition. One advantage is that one always finds the proper calibers of ammunition close at hand. Another, greater advantage is that logistical problems are reduced to a minimum. The enemy supply lines serve both armies, and often serve the guerrilla army better than they do that of the adversary.

¶ Guerrilla strategy is dynamic. It has positive political objectives and positive military goals. The strategic defensive, as Mao calls it, is an *active* defense based on incessant attack. The harrassing tactics of the guerrilla, while they bear superficial resemblance to the delaying actions fought by rear-guard regular troops, have a different purpose. It is to wear down the enemy, and to force him to over-extend his lines, so that his manpower can be annihilated, a unit at a time.

"Guerrillas can gain the initiative," writes Mao, "if they keep in mind the weak points of the enemy. Because of the enemy's insufficient manpower, guerrillas can operate over vast territories; because the enemy is a foreigner and a barbarian, guerrillas can gain the confidence of millions of their countrymen. . . .

The reference was to the Japanese invader in China, and Mao makes it clear at all times that his laws of war were meant to apply specifically to China and the Chinese situation. What he says nevertheless has a more general application. For "foreigner and barbarian" substitute "oppressor and exploiter" and the confidence of which he speaks can be gained in many countries where no question of foreign intrusion arises.

¶ *On tactics:* "In guerrilla warfare select the tactics of seeming to come from the east and attacking from the west; avoid the solid, attack the hollow; attack; withdraw; deliver a lightning blow, seak a lightning decision. . . ."

¶ *On politics:* "Without a political goal, guerrilla warfare must fail, as it must if its political objectives do not coincide with the aspirations of the people, and their sympathy, cooperation and assistance cannot be gained. The essence of guerrilla warfare is thus political in character.

"On the other hand, in a war of counterrevolutionary nature, there is no place for guerrilla hostilities. Because guerrilla warfare basically derives from the masses and is supported by them, it can neither exist nor flourish if it separates itself from their sympathies and cooperation."

Mao's rules for the conduct of guerrilla warfare are rhetorical, redundant, and often less precise than one might wish. They leave many practical questions unanswered. It is to be remembered that he was writing political documents, not a text for insurgents. His collected works remain, nevertheless, the primer of guerrilla theory; and the study of his campaigns, which ended with the destruction and defeat of any army of 3,700,000 men (the greatest in Chinese history) reveals much that is relevant elsewhere, in countries which, like China, lack arms and industry, but do not lack the basic ingredients of revolutionary war: *space*, *time*, and *will*.

# COLONIAL WAR AND THE FRENCH EXPERIENCE. STRATEGY AND TACTICS OF VO NGUYEN GIAP. HOW THE VIETMINH WON IN INDOCHINA.

How do the "laws of revolutionary war" laid down by Mao Tse-tung apply to the remaining colonies of the great powers?

The answer is implicit in the historical record. During the two decades since World War II, *no colonial war* has been lost by a colonial people, once entered into. (Malaya and the Philippines are only apparent exceptions, not real ones. They will be discussed in a later chapter.)

In the more fortunate instances, the colonial powers have ceded their authority in good time, bowing before the wind of history. Elsewhere, revolutionary action has wrested the erstwhile colonies away by the extortion of terror and civil disorder, as in Cyprus and Morocco, or by clear force of arms, as in Algeria and Indochina.

The struggle against the French colonial power in Indochina is of especial interest. In it we find the most clear-cut examples both of the sort of revolutionary war that must be fought to a military decision (as opposed to the insurgency that ends in political decision), and of a war fought consciously and even conscientiously according to Mao's precepts.

As Katzenbach remarks: ". . . the war the Vietminh [followers of Ho Chi Minh] fought in northern Indochina followed [Mao's] teachings phase by phase despite the claims of Vietminh leaders that they improved on the doctrines."

The struggle lasted from 1946, when Ho Chi Minh took up arms against a French invasion (actually he had taken virtual possession of Viet Nam the year before, with the surrender of the Japanese to British, Chinese, and native forces), until 1954, when the country was partitioned at the 17th Parallel under the terms of an international government reached at Geneva, following the fall of the French stronghold of Dien Bien Phu.

If the outcome of the war represented something less than a complete victory for the Communist Vietminh, it nevertheless spelled absolute defeat for the French, and marked the end of French rule in Viet Nam. Although the bulk of the 500,000-man French Expeditionary Corps remained intact (172,000 casualties in eight years of fighting), its spirit was broken, and the political compromise that followed failed to disguise the fact that French arms had met ignominious defeat in the field, at the hands of what had been considered a ragtag native army that could be smashed in ten weeks.

During eight years of battle, the Vietminh passed from a movement of scattered guerrilla bands, operating in company or even platoon strength, to a regular army of mobile divisions armed with light artillery and equal in organization and fighting ability to the best that the French could put into the field. But while the final phase, the strategic offensive described by Mao, was fought by such an army, by far the greater part of the long campaign was guerrilla warfare.

The definition of guerrilla warfare offered by General Vo Nguyen Giap, the victor of Dien Bien Phu, concurs with Mao's. Even the rhetoric is the same:

> Guerrilla war is the form of fighting by the masses of a weak and badly equipped country against an aggressive army with better equipment and techniques. This is the way of fighting a revolution. Guerrillas rely on heroic spirit to triumph over modern weapons, avoiding the enemy when he is the stronger and attacking him when he is the weaker. Now scattering, now regrouping, now wearing out, now exterminating the enemy, they are determined to fight everywhere, so that wherever the enemy goes he

is submerged in a sea of armed people who hit back at him, thus undermining his spirit and exhausting his forces.*

Fortunately for his cause, Giap had absorbed the practical wisdom as well as the political rhetoric of his mentor, so that he is on solid ground when he writes:

> In addition to scattering to wear out the enemy, it is necessary to regroup big armed forces in favorable situations to achieve supremacy in attack at a given point and time to annihilate the enemy. Successes in many small fights added together gradually wear out the enemy manpower, while little by little strengthening our forces. The main goal of the fight must be destruction of enemy manpower. Our own manpower should not be exhausted from trying to keep or occupy land.†

Giap's definition of his objectives is purely military. In a colonial situation, the political effects of guerrilla war are less important, perhaps, than in a war against the native government of a semi-colonial country such as Cuba. Certainly they were less important in the case of a nation defending itself against an invader—France's role after World War II. But this is to speak of the effects of the struggle on government morale and on world opinion; clearly the primary political task of militating the people retained the same vital importance in Viet Nam as anywhere, a fact which Giap himself recognizes.

Writing of the first years of the long guerrilla campaign, he says that in the beginning "there appeared a tendency not to take into due account the part played by political work, and the political workers did not yet grasp [the fact] that the main task was political education and ideological leadership."

Later, however, "the terror was perceived, and due attention was paid to the key political problem, that of uniting the nation in all its social sectors, and joining all ethnic groups in a multina-

---

*Vo Nguyen Giap, "Inside the Vietminh," in *The Guerrilla—and How to Fight Him;* slightly different translation in Vo Nguyen Giap, *People's War, People's Army.* Praeger.
†*Op. cit.*

tional country against foreign domination. The Party strove hard to avail itself of favorable opportunities to push the people into the struggle," Giap relates with considerable candor. And again: "The National United Front was to be a vast assembly of all the forces capable of being united, neutralizing all those which could be neutralized, dividing all those it was possible to divide."

Early neglect of the peasantry was quickly rectified in the face of the realities of a war in a peasant country, and agrarian reform with the slogan "Land to the Tillers" became a rallying cry of the revolution.

> The enemy of the Vietnamese nation [writes Giap] was aggressive imperialism, which had to be overthrown. But, as the imperialists had long since joined with the feudal landlords, the anti-imperialist struggle definitely could not be separated from anti-feudal action. On the other hand, in a backward colonial country such as ours, where the peasants make up the majority of the population, a people's war is essentially a peasants' war under the leadership of the working class. A general mobilization of the whole people is, therefore, neither more nor less than a mobilization of the rural masses.

The failure to form a broad popular front, especially one including the religious sects, notably the Buddhists, cost the Vietminh dearly in South Viet Nam at the beginning of the struggle. As we have noted, Ho Chi Minh's guerrilla forces had taken virtual control of the country with the surrender of the Japanese occupation forces of World War II. In part because of the defection of the religious sects, the French armored forces landing in South Viet Nam met little opposition. Within a few months, they held much of what was then called Cochinchina, Viet Nam's southernmost state, of which Saigon is the capital.

Only lack of manpower—40,000 troops under the command of General Leclerc comprised the initial expeditionary force—prevented them from seizing the flatlands of Annam and Tonkin as well.

As the French observer Dr. Bernard Fall (*Street Without Joy* and

*The Two Viet-Nams*) remarks, French objectives in Indochina in 1946 "envisioned little more than a campaign of colonial reconquest along classic lines, like Marshal Lyautey's campaign against Abd el Krim's Riff Kabyles in the 1920's."

The method chosen was the so-called "oil-slick technique." It involved the establishment of strong points in a region, from which "pacification" forces would spread out to cut the countryside into small squares and then to comb each square on the grid, working from the outside, until the rebel forces within the net were finally brought to close quarters and exterminated. It is, in effect, a police method. The trouble was that Leclerc did not have a sufficient number of policemen for the *ratissage*, the combing without which the whole plan falls to pieces.

The French campaign fit a pattern typical of what must be expected to happen when regular military forces try to combat guerrillas as though they were a conventional military enemy, or, on the other hand, treat them as mere roving bandits, to be dispersed by flying columns and picked off one by one.

Leclerc's armored columns rushed in, seized the major roads and the important crossroad towns, and felt that they had made a successful start, since they met little determined resistance at any point.

What they failed to realize initially was that, although they controlled the roads, they were fighting an enemy that had no need of roads, being without transport or heavy artillery to move. They seized strong points, but these strong points commanded nothing, since the enemy was not stationary but fluid and offered no contest for strong points or for territory.

The French controlled the roads. The guerillas passed safely in the jungle and rice paddies on either side at a distance of one hundred yards, unseen. The French held the towns. The enemy had no design on the towns. For where the French were fighting to control the national territory—that meant to occupy it—the guerrillas were interested only in winning its population. Note: this is the essential contrast between conventional war and guerrilla war. The army fights to occupy territory, roads, strategic heights, vital areas; the guerrilla fights to control people, without whose cooperation the land is useless to its possessor.

The oil-slick pattern, better for catching bandits than for fighting guerrillas, might actually have been used to some advantage in Indochina, had the French commanded more troops to devote to the campaign. But in a revolutionary situation— moreover one in which foreign troops oppose native guerrillas— the suppression campaign could only work locally. What is the method of preventing new outbreaks, short of exterminating entire populations? It has yet to be discovered. The Vietnamese casualties that fell before the French were very high, the death toll heavy during eight years of bitter internal war. Dr. Fall estimates Vietminh casualties at three times those of the French Union Forces, putting the latter at 172,000. Yet there is strong evidence that the great bulk of the native casualties were not guerrillas but civilians—innocent bystanders. [For a discussion of present-day casualties in South Viet Nam, under much the same conditions, see Chapter VI.]

The French drive was doomed to failure. The country was too big, the population was too great, and there was too much natural cover for the guerrillas; the French forces were far too small for an effort that requires a minimum ratio of ten soldiers for every guerrilla, and may very well need twenty or one hundred in a land where *every* native is a potential guerrilla fighter.

Vietminh troops were organized on three levels, according to the pattern established in China and used elsewhere. At the top were the so-called *chu-luc* regulars, permanent guerrilla fighters who could be employed strategically wherever needed and who carried the main campaign, when insurgent forces were concentrated for a major strike. Beneath the *chu-luc* were the regional guerrillas, who fought only in their own zones, and could always return to their civilian character as peasants and workers if hard pressed. And on the bottom level were the village militia, the *du-kich*, guerrillas by night and peasants by day, carrying out limited assignments—sabotaging a bridge here, ambushing a patrol there, mining the roads, carrying messages or funds—and fading back into their farms and villages at the first approach of military opposition.

"At the first shots of the imperialist invasion," writes General Giap, "General Leclerc . . . estimated that the reoccupation of

Vietnam would be a military walk-over. When encountering resistance in the South, the French generals considered it weak and temporary and stuck to their opinion that it would take ten weeks at most to occupy and pacify the whole of South Vietnam.

"Why did the French colonialists make such an estimate? Because they considered that to meet their aggression, there must be an army . . . it was not possible for them to understand a fundamental and decisive fact: the Vietnamese Army, although weak materially, was a people's army. . . . In provoking hostilities, the colonialists had alienated a whole nation. And indeed, the whole Vietnamese nation, the entire Vietnamese people, rose against them. Unable to grasp this profound truth, the French generals, who believed in an easy victory, went instead to certain defeat."

Allowing for rhetorical exaggeration, there is still much in what Giap says. The French forces, concentrating on strong points and other objectives of conventional warfare strategy, found themselves "submerged in a sea of armed people." The arms, in the main, came from the French Expeditionary Corps, which, says Giap, "became, unwittingly, the supplier of the Vietnam People's Army with French, even U.S. arms."

As for the organization of the resistance, Giap notes that it was primarily *political* and only secondarily military:

Our party advocated that, to launch the people's war, it was necessary to have three kinds of armed forces. It attached great importance to the building and development of self-defense units and guerrilla units. Militia was set up everywhere. *Thanks to the founding of [the] people's administration everywhere in the countryside, and the existence of Party branches in every place,* the militia spread far and wide and the people rose to fight. In the enemy's rear, guerrilla units, in coordination with the regular army, scattered and wore out the enemy, nailed them to their bases, so that our regular army could launch mobile fighting to annihilate them. They turned the enemy rear into our front line and built guerrilla bases as starting points for our regular army's offensive, right in the heart of the enemy. They protected the people and their property, fought the enemy and kept up production, and frustrated the enemy's schemes to use war to feed war and Vietnamese to fight Vietnamese. In the free zone, guerrilla units effectively fought the enemy and kept watch on traitors; *they were effective instruments for the local administration and local Party;* at the same time, they were the shock force in production, transport, and supply. Through combat and work, the guerrilla units became an inexhaustible and precious source of replenishment for the regular army, supplying it with men and officers who were politically well educated and rich in fighting experience. [Italics author's.]

Both sides made serious mistakes in the early phase of the eight-year struggle. The French, for their part, devoted a full five months of 1947 to the fruitless task of attempting to capture Ho Chi Minh and his staff, thinking in this way to cut short the war. The effort was wasted. Even if they had captured Ho, it probably would not have affected the course of a war, the outcome of which depended not on individual military genius but on a strategy dictated by the politico-military situation—a strategy that any Communist leader, aware of the lesson of China, would have applied.

Here it may be well to observe that, to a very great extent, guerrillas fight as they do because they must. Their situation determines their course of action. Lacking the heavy weapons and disciplined divisions with which to fight conventional military campaigns, they are confined, as Clausewitz puts it, to nibbling at the edges of the opposing army and fighting in the enemy's rear areas. Materially unable to face a military decision, they must of necessity await a political decision. In a revolutionary situation, political decisions will tend to favor their side, since these will come in the course of a protracted war which the enemy is neither politically nor psychologically able to stand, whatever the condition of his military forces.

As General Giap analyzed the situation of the French:

> The enemy will pass slowly from the offensive to the defensive. The blitzkrieg will transform itself into a war of duration. Thus, the enemy will be caught in a dilemma: He has to drag out the war in order to win it, and does not possess, on the other hand, the psychological and political means to fight a long-drawn-out war. . . .

Giap, of course, proved to be correct. Political pressures in France, the low morale of the pro-French sector of public opinion in Viet Nam, and the sagging morale of the troops themselves as the war dragged on, seriously weakened the efforts of the Expeditionary Corps.

The country was swarming with guerrilla militia; units were organized in virtually every village. Vietminh regulars were making rapid forced marches through the jungle to strike a French column here, a small garrison there, and were rapidly arming new units with weapons seized from the enemy, as well as heavier equipment smuggled from China.

By the end of 1949, the French had lost the initiative and the Vietminh had seized it to such an extent that the latter were able to launch a limited offensive with fifteen battalions, sealing off part of the Red River delta in Tonkin from the Thai highlands.

In the spring, a larger offensive was launched against French defenses in the Red River Valley, and by summer the entire northeastern corner of Tonkin had been converted into a Vietminh stronghold.

Political pressures in France predictably worked for the Vietminh. In August, 1950, the French government actually ordered a *reduction* of the French forces in Indochina by 9,000 troops, ignoring the military realities of the situation there entirely; and the National Assembly, yielding to popular anti-war sentiment at home, required assurances that no military conscripts would be used in Indochina. In other words, it was to be a police action carried out by professionals, principally Foreign Legion, Moroccan, and other non-French troops.

The inevitable result was a further weakening of the French war effort, and a new offensive on the part of the Vietminh. An entire string of garrisons in northern Tonkin were cut off from their base. A Moroccan task force of 3,500 men and a garrison force of 2,600 men and 500 civilians seeking to escape from the entrapment were ambushed and destroyed; and three battalions of paratroopers sent to their rescue met the same fate.

In *The Two Viet-Nams*, Bernard Fall writes:

> By the end of the month of October, 1950, almost the whole northern half of Viet-Nam had become a Vietminh redoubt, into

which the French were—with the brief exception of a paratroop raid on Lang-Song in July, 1953—never to penetrate again. . . .

When the smoke had cleared, the French had suffered their greatest colonial defeat since Montcalm had died at Quebec. They had lost 6,000 troops, 13 artillery pieces and 125 mortars, 450 trucks and three armored platoons, 940 machineguns, 1,200 sub-machineguns, and more than 8,000 rifles. Their abandoned stocks alone sufficed for the equipment of a whole . . . Viet-Minh division.*

"For the French," Fall concludes, "the Indochina War was lost then and there. That it was allowed to drag on inconclusively for another four years is a testimony to the shortsightedness of the civilian authorities who were charged with drawing the political conclusions from the hopeless military situation. American military aid—the first trickle of which had made its appearance in the form of seven transport planes in June, 1950, after the Korean War had broken out—was to make no difference whatever in the eventual outcome of the war."

The progress of the Vietminh was slowed to some extent by General Giap's premature decision, at the end of 1950, to begin a general offensive. The attempt to force the campaign into Mao's decisive third stage of revolutionary war, the strategic offensive, when the situation was not yet ripe, cost the Vietminh heavily. In a single clash in the Red River delta area, January 16–17, Giap lost 6,000 men. When he tried to seize the port of Haiphong in March, 1951, he was again defeated. And in June, a third drive for control of the delta likewise failed.

Thereafter, the Vietminh wisely transferred their efforts to more promising objectives; in particular, to control of the highland areas, where heavy artillery, air power, and armor could not be brought fully into play, and the French had to fight on the Vietminh's terms.

The key military problem of the French in Indochina was lack of manpower; their main political problem was lack of support on the home front. Diplomatic pressures added to these problems. Vietminh strategy was flexible; that of the French was

*Frederick A. Praeger, Inc., Publishers.

comparatively rigid, so that time and again the Expeditionary Corps was caught off balance.

Lack of manpower meant that too few troops were required to cover too much territory, with the result that the Corps was unable to meet the lightning blows of fast-moving Vietminh mobile divisions when these concentrated for an offensive. And when the French themselves went on the offensive and tried to concentrate their forces to seize the initiative in a given sector, Vietminh guerrilla action elsewhere along the line made them spread out again. Moreover, Vietminh strategy, being political as well as military, was designed to increase the political and psychological pressure on the enemy, and was signally successful in accomplishing this objective.

The point is well illustrated by Giap's invasion of Laos in the early spring of 1953. The invasion was launched with three Vietminh divisions, supported internally by some 4,000 Pathet-Lao guerrillas. In opposition were only 3,000 French troops, backed by the Laotian Army of 10,000 men.

Rather than sacrifice the thinly manned frontier garrisons, the French command ordered them to withdraw, leaving only a single battalion to offer rear-guard resistance. The battalion was lost; only four men survived. Another garrison retreating inland lost all but 180 of its 2,400 troops in a disastrous fighting withdrawal.

Reinforcements airlifted into Laos from Viet Nam stemmed the invasion on the Plaine des Jarres, but at the cost of further depleting the French reserves in the main area of hostilities and tying up all available French air transport. The Vietminh were beaten back, but the campaign was, from their point of view, far from a wasted effort.

As Katzenbach comments in "Time, Space, and Will":

> . . . the results of this action, whether the whole of the intended result was achieved or not, were as far-reaching as if a major victory had been won. Seldom has so much been accomplished with so little.
>
> Perhaps in the cold light of afterthought, the most curious aspect of the whole action was that from the beginning it made

a mockery of the old saying, "Nothing risked; nothing gained." Whatever the gain, no military investment of sizable proportions was risked. This was quite as safe a venture, in a word, as the Chinese invasion of Tibet.

Yet after a three-week invasion, this is what the Communists had accomplished: (1) They had thrown terror into the French (military and civil authorities alike) in both Indochina and metropolitan France; (2) they had spread French defending forces in Indochina even thinner than previously; (3) they had produced renewed demands for a larger measure of political autonomy in both Laos and nearby Cambodia; (4) they had created a situation in which French spending in the area was raised by some $60 million; and (5) they had cost the United States some $460 million extra by way of foreign aid.

One of the most interesting accounts of revolutionary warfare that has been written is Vo Nguyen Giap's own account of the Vietminh strategy used to block the well-publicized Navarre Plan—France's last-gasp effort, as it turned out, to regain the military initiative in Indochina.

The plan conceived by the latest of a succession of French commanders-in-chief, General Henri Navarre, envisioned a strategic offensive designed, as the late John Foster Dulles assured a committee of the United States Senate, to "break the organized body of Communist aggression* by the end of the 1955 fighting season [in eighteen months]."

Navarre conceded privately, in a secret report not published until long after the battle of Dien Bien Phu, that the war in Indochina was already lost when the Navarre Plan went into effect; the best that could be hoped for, even at that time, was a stalemate.

Be that as it may, the Plan was put into operation, with powerful financial and material assistance from the United States.

---

*Note the phrase, "Communist aggression"—this after the Vietnamese had been fighting a French *invasion* for more than seven years. But Dulles' attitude toward the struggle, in which perhaps 200,000 Vietnamese lives were lost, is betrayed by the sportsman's reference to "the 1955 fighting season." Everything has its season, even fighting Communist "aggression" and killing Vietnamese.

Navarre's strategy was to concentrate strong mobile forces in the Red River delta in an effort to engage and wear down the main body of the Vietminh, during the fall and winter of 1953, while at the same time occupying Dien Bien Phu, to the west, as a springboard from which to launch powerful stabs at Communist free zones in the surrounding area. With the spring of 1954, the Vietminh presumably being exhausted by this time, the French were to speed other, newly formed units to seize Vietminh free zones in South Viet Nam, this mop-up to be followed by a general offensive in the North that would bring the war to a successful conclusion.

Forty-four French mobile battalions were concentrated in the Red River delta for the first phase of this operation, during the fall of 1953, and a series of fierce battles followed. In January, French paratroopers occupied Dien Bien Phu and a powerful buildup there began.

The Vietminh, meanwhile, launched their counter-offensive, encircling Dien Bien Phu, joining forces with the Pathet Lao for a stab into upper Laos, followed in January by an offensive in the western highlands and two further thrusts into Laos, one in the south and the other in the north, the latter liberating the Nam Hu basin and threatening the Laotian capital, Luang Prabang.

In March, as the French regrouped to resume their own offensive, the Vietminh opened their historic 55-day assault on Dien Bien Phu.

"The strategic direction of the Dien Bien Phu campaign and of the winter 1953–spring 1954 campaign in general," writes General Giap, "was a typical success of the revolutionary military line of Marxism-Leninism applied to the actual conditions of the revolutionary war in Viet Nam."

Our strategy started from thorough analysis of the enemy's contradictions. It aimed at concentrating our forces in the enemy's relatively exposed sectors, annihilating their manpower, liberating a part of the territory, and compelling them to scatter their forces, thus creating favorable conditions for a decisive victory.

For the French Expeditionary Corps, the war was a continuous process of dispersal of forces. The enemy divisions were split into regiments, then into battalions, companies, and platoons, to be stationed at thousands of points and posts on the various battle fronts of the Indochina theatre of operations. The enemy found himself face to face with a contradiction. Without scattering his forces, it would be impossible for him to occupy the invaded territory; in scattering his forces, he put himself in difficulties. The scattered units would fall easy prey to our troops, their mobile forces would be more and more reduced, and the shortage of troops would be all the more acute. On the other hand, if they concentrated their forces to move from the defensive position and cope with us with more initiative, the occupation forces would be weakened and it would be difficult for them to hold the invaded territory. *Now, if the enemy gives up occupied territory, the very aim of the war of reconquest is defeated.* [Italics author's.]

The objectives of the Navarre plan have already been stated. In preparing to put the plan into operation, the French found themselves faced with a dilemma: they could not go on the offensive without concentrating their manpower, yet would be unable to defend the many weak links in the strategic chain of defensive posts if they did concentrate it. Lack of manpower was the crippling factor. To make up for the deficiency, new units were formed (many consisted of Vietnamese recruits, or, as the Vietminh insisted, mercenaries), and existing units stationed at posts that were considered "static" were secretly shifted for the big build-up in the Red River delta.

Needless to say, the Navarre Plan confronted the Vietminh with the necessity of making serious decisions, too. Giap recounts the dilemma:

The concrete problem was: The enemy was concentrating in the Red River delta, and launching attacks on our free zones. Now, should we concentrate our forces to face the enemy, or mobilize them for attacks in other directions? . . . In concentrating our forces to fight the enemy in the Delta, we could defend our free zone; but here the enemy was still strong and we could easily be decimated. On the other hand, in attacking in other directions with our main forces, we could exploit the vulnerable points of the enemy to annihilate the bulk of their forces; but our free zone would thus be threatened.

The Communist Party's Central Committee put its collective mind to the problem, Giap soberly relates, and came up with a *slogan:* "Dynamism, initiative, mobility, and rapidity of decision in the face of new situations." While less than informative, the slogan did have meaning, as Giap explains:

> Keeping the initiative, we should concentrate our forces to attack strategic points which were relatively vulnerable. If we succeeded in keeping the initiative, we could achieve successes and compel the enemy to scatter their forces. . . . On the other hand, if we were driven on the defensive, not only could we not annihilate many enemy forces, but our own force could easily suffer losses. . . .

A dynamic campaign that was decided upon.

> Always convinced that the essential thing was to destroy the enemy's manpower, the Central Committee worked out its plan of action by scientific analysis: to concentrate our offense against important strategic points where the enemy were relatively weak in order to wipe out a part of their manpower, at the same time compelling them to scatter their forces to cope with us at vital points which they had to defend at all costs.
> This strategy proved correct. While the enemy was concentrating big forces in the Delta to threaten our free zone, instead of leaving our main forces in the Delta or scattering our forces in the free zone to defend it by a defensive action, we regrouped our forces and boldly attacked in the direction of the northwest.

The result was the destruction, says Giap, of "thousands of local bandits (armed by the French)" and the liberation of four strategic strong points, the destruction of the greater part of a French column, and the encirclement of Dien Bien Phu, "thus compelling the enemy to carry out in haste a reinforcement movement to save it from being wiped out." Giap adds a significant observation: "In addition to the Red River Delta, Dien Bien Phu [thus] became a second point of concentration of enemy forces."

At the same time, the Middle Laos offensive was in progress, forcing the French to rush more reinforcements in another direction and so to weaken further the build-up in the delta, while creating a third point of concentration at the threatened air base of Seno.

Further diversions were created, including a Vietminh assault on the western highlands and the offensive in Upper Laos, sending French reinforcement speeding in two new directions.

> For us [writes Giap] the first phase of the winter-spring campaign was a series of offensives launched simultaneously on various important sectors where the enemy were relatively exposed, in which we annihilated part of the enemy's forces and liberated occupied areas, at the same time compelling the enemy to scatter their forces in many directions. We continually kept the initiative in the operations and drove the enemy on the defensive . . . On the main battlefront, we pinned down the enemy at Dien Bien Phu, thus creating favorable conditions for our troops on other battlefields.

The result of the Vietminh strategy was to relieve pressure on the free zones, to such an extent that "our compatriots could go to work . . . even in daytime without being molested by enemy aircraft," and to keep the French too busy and too scattered for the local mopping-up operations which the Navarre Plan had envisioned as the prelude to a general offensive against the main body of Vietminh forces in the North. In consequence, guerrilla areas behind the French lines in South Viet Nam were never eliminated, and with this constant threat, added to the pressure on encircled Dien Bien Phu, French hopes of regaining the initiative quickly faded.

The Navarre Plan was smashed before it could be fairly put into operation. The destruction of the fortified camp at Dien Bien Phu and the surrender of what remained of its garrison—at full strength it had consisted of seventeen infantry battalions, three artillery battalions, plus various engineer tank units and paratroops, defending forty-nine concrete strongposts—was the decisive blow.

The battle lasted for fifty-five days. "At 0153 local time, on

May 8, 1954," writes Bernard Fall, "the last guns fell silent at Dien Bien Phu after a desperate bayonet charge of the Algerian and Foreign Legion garrison of strongpoint 'Isabelle' had been smothered by sheer numbers of the victorious Viet-Minh, and the war that had lasted eight years was almost over."

A military survey team sent to Saigon from France to learn the extent of the disaster recommended that the French abandon North Viet Nam as a lost cause and, if they could, hold the area below the 17th Parallel. The diplomatic settlement in Geneva that followed, bringing peace to Viet Nam—but not permanent peace—ratified the military decision.

"The Indochina War ended on July 21, 1954, at 0343," writes Fall, ever precise. "It had cost the French Union Forces a total of 172,000 casualties and forever broken France's hold on Viet-Nam."

# THE POLITICAL CHARACTER OF THE SECOND INDOCHINA WAR. THE AMERICAN ROLE. EXPANSION OF THE WAR. THE OUTLOOK.

The silence that follows the fall of Dien Bien Phu is but a moment in the span of history, an all too brief breathing spell. Scarcely five years separate the First Indochina War, as Bernard Fall calls it, from the start of the Second. Since then, events have made Viet Nam again the focal point of global concern, the storm center around which swirls a vast political conflict, a clash of ideologies and empires that could easily produce a major war in Asia.

Yet from a certain Vietnamese point of view, little seems to have changed in the essential situation. To the South Vietnamese peasant looking up from his rice paddies, the warplanes that whine overhead on their way to distant targets in the North, the helicopters clattering toward some battle rendezvous, are indistinguishable from the planes and helicopters that carried French troops into battle against the Vietminh a decade ago. To a Communist guerrilla in the brush or in the villages, today's battle is like that of yesterday and last year and the year before that; the war is all of a piece, and many young men cannot remember when there was no war.

American uniforms have replaced French uniforms in Saigon; directives come from Washington instead of Paris. The Vietminh are now called the Viet Cong; and the new invaders, for a long while given the courtesy title of "military advisers" but now finally acknowledged to be combatants, are called Americans. It makes little difference: French or Americans, Vietminh or Viet Cong, the war goes on, both sides pursuing the same objectives as before, by the same familiar methods. It is the struggle of dog and flea; and the flea continues, slowly but inevitably, to multiply and to win.

A United Press International news analysis of March 24, 1965, disclosing in a few telling paragraphs the dilemma of the American forces in Viet Nam, could almost have been written a decade earlier, with respect to the French situation of that time.

> The United States is now deep into the fourth year of an increasingly bloody battle for this land of mountains, jungles, rice paddies, and Communist guerrillas.
>
> Since May 1961, when the United States first committed itself to support the anti-Communist Saigon government,* it has poured in vast quantities of men and machines.
>
> From rifles to rockets, from jeeps to tanks, from helicopters to jet bombers, the United States has moved in billions of dollars worth of the most sophisticated weapons in its arsenal.
>
> It has given freely of its brains, its blood, and its lives. All has been to no avail. The world's mightiest nation has been unable to find the key to success in Southeast Asia.
>
> From the day it set foot in this unhappy land, the United States course in the fight against Communists has been downhill.
>
> . . . When the war in South Vietnam began, the rebels operated in no more than platoon strength. They were able to ambush a truck here, or knock over an isolated outpost there.
>
> But as they accumulated American weapons from the bodies of the government dead, they replaced their homemade firearms and recruited young men to make their platoons into companies.
>
> The Viet Cong claim to have liberated more than three-quarters of the total territory of the nation, and to have established schools, hospitals, and public works.
>
> The Viet Cong have designated the cities as the last strongholds of the Saigon regime and its American masters—and the

---

*But this is to overlook the fact that the United States was supplying the French with war materiel even before Dien Bien Phu, footing the cost of the Indochina war to the extent of $1,250,000,000.

fact is that the government troops do spend much of their time in the relative safety of urban areas. They are ferried out in heli-copters. When they take to the roads, it is in armored cars and tanks. Still they are ambushed.

Using the Communist technique of two steps forward, one step back, the Viet Cong practices a flexibility in tactics that the government has never been able to achieve.*

By all the signs, it is a desperate military situation—far more desperate than that of the French during the siege of Dien Bien Phu. It goes far to explain the desperation of Washington's re-sponses, beginning with air raids on supposed Viet Cong supply lines in the North and rapidly escalating, by the spring of 1965, to a sustained aerial offensive against a wide variety of "targets of opportunity" deep in North Viet Nam.

As late as March 25, 1965, President Lyndon Johnson took oc-casion to declare: "The United States still seeks no wider war. We threaten no regime and covet no territory. We have worked and will continue to work for a reduction of tensions on the great stage of the world."

But both Hanoi and Peking clearly *felt* threatened by the American military buildup and the continuing air offensive. Nor was the anxiety theirs alone. French President DeGaulle had long been pressing for a negotiated settlement of the war. In London, March 23, Prime Minister Harold Wilson said that Brit-ain would ask an explanation of a statement attributed to U.S. Ambassador Maxwell Taylor in Saigon, to the effect that the United States would, if need be, wage war "without limit" in Viet Nam.

Johnson's declaration of peaceful intentions failed to reassure a worried world. The President asserted that the United States sought no wider war, but added in the same breath: "This is no struggle of white men against Asians. It is aggression by Com-munist totalitarians against their independent neighbors . . . the aggression from the North must be stopped. That is the road to peace in Southwest Asia."

*Arthur J. Dommen, "Great Decisions—1965," United Press International Series.

The implicit denial of the existence of a civil war in South Viet Nam, a territory already three-quarters in the hands of Viet Cong guerrillas, the insistence on blaming "Communist totalitarians . . . aggression from the North," with clear reference to North Viet Nam and China, suggested an obvious, ominous conclusion.

The United States, unable to win in South Viet Nam, seemed all too clearly to be preparing to expand the struggle into a broader arena in which American technological superiority would count for more—a Korean War situation in which the American public would perforce support a new, full-scale crusade against Communism in the Orient.

The ostensible object of the air offensive against North Viet Nam was to force Hanoi, perhaps also Peking, to negotiate a settlement, a return, as Johnson put it, "to the essentials of the agreements of 1954—a reliable arrangement to guarantee the independence and security of all in Southeast Asia." But since Hanoi and Peking, even if supporting the Viet Cong, were scarcely in a position to dictate terms to guerrillas on the brink of victory in South Viet Nam, talk of negotiations could hardly be taken seriously.

The situation confronting the Pentagon in March of 1965 was well summarized by the Washington columnist Marquis Childs on March 25, 1965:

> The headlines from day to day concentrate on American bombing of North Vietnam. They divert attention from the grim fact fundamental to the conflict and American involvement:
> The war on the ground in South Vietnam is rapidly being lost.
> So far-reaching is the control of the Viet Cong guerrillas that it has become all but impossible to supply outlying provinces except by transport planes.
> Increasingly by the United States bombing in South Vietnam and the use of napalm* the Vietnamese people in the south are being alienated. . . .
> It is becoming more and more certain that American ground troops in division strength will have to be committed to Vietnam

* At the same time, the use of *gas* created a new scandal.

if the war is not to end in disastrous defeat. On the eve of his visit to Washington to report to President Johnson, Ambassador Maxwell Taylor said almost as much.

The point of no return on the road to full-scale direct American commitment to carry on the war on the ground and in the air seems, therefore, to be at hand.

\*    \*    \*

How did this situation develop, and why?

In order to consider the conflict in Viet Nam with any degree of clarity, it is necessary for Americans to digest some unpalatable facts—unpalatable because we are accustomed to think of ourselves as democrats, anticolonialists, libertarians, not as imperialists, never as aggressors.

The painful fact is that, from the Vietnamese point of view, the Second Indochina War is a direct continuation of the First. Politically it continues to be a struggle for territorial independence and freedom from foreign, or at any rate Western, domination; socially it continues to be a socialist, i.e., Marxist, revolution, aimed at destroying an economic system that is compatible with our own and replacing it with one that, as it happens, is not.

In the effort to block the process, the United States assumed the position of the French colonial power in South Viet Nam, and adopted similar methods in pursuit of parallel goals. History is unlikely to make the fine distinction between French colonialists and American "anti-Communists." The distinction between French soldiers and American "military advisers" will certainly be lost. What remains clear is that where the French sought to retain Viet Nam as a colony—part of their once vast sphere of influence—the United States seeks to secure it as a satellite; that is, as part of an Asian domain that we deem essential to American interests, responsive to us economically, politically, above all militarily.

This is to describe events in a single area of a worldwide power struggle. World War II destroyed the old spheres of influence and the old balance of power; the First Indochina War was a part of that disintegration. A realignment is now in progress, with the so-called Third World, the undeveloped world of former colonies, as the field of combat and object of contention. What does not come into the American orbit will fall—so we fear—into the Communist (Chinese or Russian) orbits. Hence our concern with South Viet Nam and our assumption of the French role in that country.

"The stakes in Southeast Asia are large," asserted *The New York Times* of May 24, 1964. "If Laos and South Vietnam should fall to the Communists, they would likely take with them Cambodia, Thailand and Burma, possibly even Malaysia and the Philippines—close to 115 million people."

The loss of South Viet Nam, said former President Eisenhower, would mean "a tremendous loss of prestige—the loss of the whole subcontinent of Southeast Asia."

Joseph Alsop wrote: "If defeat in South Viet Nam is passively accepted, all admit that this defeat will be the worst and most costly that the U.S. has submitted to in this century." And from *Life,* June 12, 1964: ". . . abandoning Southeast Asia would be a disaster. The Communist forces would take over. The U.S. would have demonstrated that it lacks the skill to win a guerrilla war and the guts to back its promises to its allies. U.S. military lines would retreat to Okinawa; Japan and the Philippines would be endangered; Indonesia would be out of control, and U.S. influence in Asia, as a practical matter, would come to an end."

These views were endorsed in official Washington. As Secretary of Defense Robert S. McNamara said in a policy statement: "The survival of an independent [read U.S.-oriented] Government in South Viet Nam is so important to the security of Southeast Asia and to the free world that I can conceive of no alternative other than to take all measures within our capability to prevent a Communist victory."

The late President Kennedy termed Southeast Asia vital to the United States as a Pacific power, and as early as June, 1964, President Johnson had declared that the United States would risk war, meaning with China, in defense of the area.

The American commitment continued to widen and deepen. By May of 1965, some 45,000 Americans were serving in the Vietnamese theater, as compared with just 685 in 1959. Direct military and economic aid to the Saigon government had risen by the end of the year to $700 million annually—with a total commitment of *five and a half billions* since 1954.*

The war goes on, with the Americans in the role once occupied by the French. There are, however, vital differences. Most of them work to the advantage of the Communists.

Washington's political and psychological inability to call a spade a spade put the United States in an awkward position for fighting what was still essentially a colonial war. Instead of a direct chain of command, there was an unreliable native government (or series of governments) in Saigon, and a Vietnamese general staff to which the American military staff stood in the relationship of "adviser." Where the burden of the war formerly was carried by the troops of the intervening foreign power— French Foreign Legionnaires, North Africans, and so on (mainly foreigners who stood above Vietnamese politics)—it had now to be left to some 400,000 native troops, Vietnamese who, like the rest of the population of their country, had minds of their own and did not necessarily view the war in the same light, or with the same objectives, as the Americans.

The French were not engaged in a popularity contest in Viet Nam. They were military men and frank colonialists, confident of their patriotic mission. Their war was military, and they had little fear of losing it in the field.

The departure of the French and the assumption of their role by the Americans marked an important political transition. The Saigon government, while clearly an instrument of American policy and a military dictatorship in the bargain, was not in the comparatively independent position of a foreign military gov-

---

*"Five and one half billion dollars worth of aid to South Vietnam, 18,000 American 'advisors,' and now the threat of war with China has not put Humpty Dumpty back together—and never will. Out of this $5$^1$/2 billion, $1$^1$/4 billion went to France to help her in the Indochina war prior to her withdrawing in 1954. Today we are spending better than $1$^1$/2 million per day and will reach $2 million shortly, just as aid to Vietnam, not covering the cost of our own military force in Southeast Asia. Unless the American people make their voices heard very soon, they are going to spend even more in this fruitless and unavailing task."—Senator Wayne Morse of Oregon in the United States Senate, August 5, 1964.

ernment commanding an army of occupation. It was compelled to take account of public opinion, to retain the confidence not only of its banker, the United States, but also of that sector of the Vietnamese populace that supported or tolerated it, including the large, burdensome army and its intrigue-ridden officers' corps.

The instability of such puppet regimes in a guerrilla war situation is revealed by the record: no fewer than nine successive governments, starting with the Ngo Dinh Diem regime, have been overthrown since 1963, and the tenth is no stronger than its predecessors.

In fostering the pretense that the Saigon authorities of the moment constituted an independent government, of which the United States was merely an ally, helpfully supplying the means to resist "aggression from the North," Washington suffered a serious loss of control, and was exposed to political pressures from which the French, though hag-ridden by their own domestic political problems, had been relatively immune.

Military reverses, an unpopular draft, religious rivalries, student riots, the intrigue of ambitious generals, war weariness—any of a number of complicated factors could tip the delicate political balance and leave the Pentagon with a war to conduct and no representation in Saigon, that is, no one to do the fighting. Small wonder if the military men on the Potomac fervently wished to expand the war, to bring their own reliable forces into it in full war strength, and so (the military reasoning would go) to regain control of it, free at last from the sticky ooze of Oriental politics.

Whatever the ultimate decision with regard to massive American intervention, it was amply clear by the end of 1964 that the war against the guerrillas in South Viet Nam could not be won by the means heretofore pursued—and might very easily be lost.

The course of the insurgency in South Viet Nam, having little to do with Hanoi until it had reached its critical phase, and even less to do with Peking except in an ideological way, has followed the classic pattern of the First Indochina War.

Isolated acts of terrorism and sporadic attacks on remote military or police posts, beginning as early as 1955, could not have been controlled except by calling out the army in full force. Yet the Diem regime could not make such a response without confessing that all was not well with the country, and did not find it politically expedient to make the admission. Instead, Diem played ostrich, pretending that the "bandits" were under control, and hoping that the national police would soon justify the pretense.

By the time the magnitude of the Viet Cong threat was realized, the guerrillas had already gained formidable strength and were fully competent to cope with the Vietnamese army, even backed by American arms, aircraft, and advisers. Progressive increases in the amount of United States military and economic aid to the Saigon government at all times lagged far behind the needs of the actual situation.

By mid-1964, attacks in platoon strength had given way to organized assaults in battalion or even in regimental strength, and the Viet Cong had grown from a few scattered guerrilla bands to an army of more than 140,000, counting both *chu-luc* regulars and auxiliaries.

Neil Sheehan of the United Press International reported on April 27, 1964: "From a few scattered bands backed by a fairly extensive secret political organization, the Communist Viet Cong have built a formidable fighting force of 40,000 men. They are organized into 45 battalions throughout the country. They are supported by *well over* 100,000 less well armed but still effective local and regional guerrillas."

Strong rear-base areas had been established and the Saigon government had been virtually isolated from the rural population, comprising 85 percent of a nation of nearly sixteen million people spread over a land area of some 127,000 square miles.

Outside of the big centers of population, the guerrillas were virtually unchallenged in much of the country, unmolested except by aircraft and occasionally by big, helicopter-borne expeditionary forces, stabbing in the dark, seeking needles in a haystack. Government armored columns were able to enter Viet Cong areas, but not without danger of ambush, and not with any hope of remaining or exercising authority over the people.

Most of the major arteries and almost all of the secondary

roads had been cut; some provincial capitals were accessible only by air; and a ring of insurgent bases around Saigon created an atmosphere of siege even in the capital, with battles sometimes mounted within six or eight miles of the city.

The Viet Cong maintained a viable rural economy in its own areas, and Viet Cong tax collectors gathered important revenues from the commerce still continuing between the insurgent zones and the cities, to such an extent that in some cases even the gasoline used to transport government troops to battle had already been taxed by the Communists while on its way to the barracks.

American economic aid to Saigon, exclusive of military aid, was put at some $241 million annually; its object, to improve the agricultural economy and win the support of the rural population. But the director of operations of the Agency for International Development (A.I.D.), James Killen, estimated that 10 to 15 percent of the total went to "twilight areas" that might be government-controlled one day and in the hands of the Viet Cong the next.

On August 15, 1964, *The New York Times* reported: "Control over an area can change overnight. In many parts of the country, American field workers complete a technical aid project, a bridge, road, or well, only to have the guerrillas occupy the village the moment the Americans and their Vietnamese co-workers pull out."

\*   \*   \*

What had happened in South Viet Nam recalled the experiences of China, and, in another hemisphere, of Cuba. The insurgents had established a competing economic and political system, dividing the national territory, and although the army might still go where it chose—but always in strong force—it could not remain without spreading itself too thin to resist concentrated guerrilla attacks. Thus the troops were increasingly restricted to their garrisons in the larger towns and cities, and increasingly made impotent.

"Clear and hold" operations, patterned on the French oil-slick technique, failed to remedy the situation, for the obvious reasons. The "clear and hold" strategy is always doomed to failure because the government, while strong enough to clear any given area temporarily, cannot hold many such areas without dangerously scattering its forces. In the face of a determined "clear and hold" drive, the guerrillas simply withdraw and redouble their activities elsewhere. Considering that the South Vietnamese army, if evenly dispersed over the national territory, would have about three armed men to each square mile, it is easy to see why "clear and hold" could not succeed against the Viet Cong, 140,000 strong and supported by virtually the entire rural population.

Here Saigon and its American military advisers encountered the French dilemma so well grasped by Giap: If they scattered their forces, they became too weak to defend themselves, and their manpower was destroyed piecemeal. Yet if they concentrated their strength, they surrendered the territory which it was their purpose to occupy, for victory could mean nothing if not the occupation of the national territory.

> More than 3,000 Government troops today slogged through flooded rice paddies . . . in a suspected Communist stronghold 35 miles northwest of Saigon in one of the biggest and most fruitless operations of the Vietnamese war.
>
> The *one* Red the troops located wounded a Vietnamese soldier with a shotgun *and escaped.*

The news item reflected a typical situation. As in most insurgencies, the guerrillas were able to choose their targets and to accept or reject combat at will. The government, lacking the military intelligence that popular support provides, found itself groping in the dark, engaged in random, hit-or-miss operations that were inordinately expensive for the results achieved. A news dispatch of April 21, 1964, provides more evidence of the same weakness:

> One group of today's Government statistics indicated the frustrations of this war. Government small-unit operations such as searches or probes by patrols reached a peak of 5,190 during the week. The spokesman said that no more than 70 of these actually had made contact.

"Contact," let it be pointed out, does not necessarily imply any further success.

As I have already noted, the Saigon government put itself under a severe handicap and gave its opposition a long head start by refusing to admit, for some years, that significant armed opposition existed in South Viet Nam. Isolated clashes with guerrillas were dismissed as the activities of a neglible remnant of Vietminh diehards still in the country, and it was not until five years later that the Ngo regime was finally forced to concede the by then undeniable fact that a full-grown insurgency was in progress.

The Viet Cong, meanwhile, had been building a powerful underground political apparatus and organizing guerrilla units on village and regional levels for the struggle to come. The early strategy of the movement was aimed at breaking the chain of political command from Saigon to the rural areas, isolating the government from the population of some 17,000 hamlets and 8,000 villages by subverting, kidnapping, or assassinating local officials—in particular, village chiefs and members of village councils. The campaign was begun in 1957, when more than 700 officials were killed, and was sharply stepped up in 1959, continuing through 1963 despite government efforts to halt it, and accounting altogether for an estimated 13,000 lives.

With political liaison between the capital and the villages effectively broken, the guerrillas began to build their army. Despite political statements about aid from "aggressors in the North," the simple fact is that probably 90 percent of Viet Cong arms consist of American weapons captured from the government troops.

Saigon's own statistics acknowledge that the Viet Cong captured 4,853 weapons during 1960, while losing only 921 weapons in action, for a net gain of 3,932, sufficient to arm a regiment. In 1962, the insurgents captured 52,000 weapons and lost 4,850, and in 1963 the gain was 83,000, the loss only 5,400, the totals representing a net gain for the Viet Cong over a two-year period of 128,682 weapons of all types, a number almost equal to the total of insurgents in all of South Viet Nam.

According to the Associated Press, quoted by I. F. Stone's Bi-Weekly of May 13, 1963:

Q. How does the Vietcong get its weapons?

A. Most Vietcong weapons are new U.S. military weapons, captured in ambushes on Government units and attacks on outposts. Often a Vietcong unit is organized initially with *no* weapons. The political organizer tells his men and women they must fight at first with handmade arms—spears, daggers, swords, and crude shotguns. To get better weapons, the unit must capture them from the enemy. The system evidently works. Vietcong arms now include modern recoilless cannon, heavy mortars, good machine guns, and very large supplies of submachine guns.

As indicated above, most of the Viet Cong's arms were seized in small-unit engagements. Government casualties, too, mounted as the result of many, many such small, scattered attacks, launched wherever superior position and superior numbers gave the Viet Cong assurance of easy victories. Insurgent operations in battalion force were rare until late in 1963, and it was not until well into 1964 that the Viet Cong began to engage in isolated set-piece battles of a conventional sort, on occasion abandoning guerrilla tactics for local tests of strength. The change of tactics, while not yet a consistent pattern, was an important indicator, serving notice that the war was slipping into a new phase, from the period of the strategic defensive, so called, to the stage in which an equilibrium of forces is reached and the government loses the military initiative to the insurgents.

Throughout 1964 the Viet Cong showed itself increasingly capable of standing and fighting when occasion demanded, with results often disastrous to the government forces:

Casualty figures disclosed today showed that the South Vietnamese Government suffered its worst losses last week in the war against the Communist guerrillas.

A spokesman for the United States Military Advisory Command said that casualties among Saigon's forces in the week starting April 12 totaled 1,000. The total consisted of 200 killed in

action, 600 wounded, and 140 captured or missing in action. . . .
During the week 26 American casualties were reported, including
one death in action.

The week included a five-day operation in the southern Me-
kong Delta near the post of Kien Long. That operation produced
some of the fiercest, most prolonged fighting of the war. The five-
day battle, which started with a Vietcong attack on Kien Long,
was declared officially ended Thursday afternoon when Government forces finally lost contact with the guerrillas.

—*The New York Times,* April 22, 1964.

Communist guerrillas attacked five government outposts and
sank a landing craft in weekend action near the Cambodian border, leaving as many as 46 South Vietnamese soldiers dead or
missing, it was announced. The Viet Cong also captured large
supplies of Government arms and ammunition.

—United Press International, May 18, 1964.

A mass airborne assault Wednesday against a Vietcong jungle
stronghold 40 miles northwest of Saigon found the base evacu-
ated. The Vietcong, with their "shadow government" reaching
into cities and villages through most of South Vietnam, had apparently once again been forewarned.

At the weekend, the offensive was continuing with a sweep of
the general area by 7,000 Vietnamese troops. Only light contact
was reported, however, and the whole operation was sharpening
doubts within the U.S. advisory command about the efficacy of
large-scale assaults against an elusive enemy.

—*The New York Times,* November 22, 1964.

In a lightning predawn strike, Communist Viet Cong guerrillas
swarmed from the mountain jungles northwest of Saigon yesterday and overran a major district capital. . . . In Washington, President Johnson ordered urgent consultations with the Saigon
government to improve in all aspects the war against the Viet
Cong.

—United Press International, December 2, 1964.

The scale of the fighting through 1964 indicated that the Communists were rapidly gaining the military initiative.

"When the United States military buildup began in South

Vietnam in November, 1961," reported United Press International, "the situation had been considered 'critical' because the Vietcong had become strong enough to initiate no fewer than 1,782 attacks and small-scale incidents in that month. But in November, 1963, after two years of massive American military and economic aid, the number of Vietcong attacks and incidents jumped to 3,182 for the month."

The continuing buildup was reported in December to have *doubled* the size of the South Vietnamese air force, but the results were by no means in ratio to the increase in striking power. As reported in *The New York Times* of December 3:

> Government air raids against insurgent concentrations have forced Communist commanders to make adjustments in battle tactics, but have not noticeably lowered their morale or fighting capability, according to a new intelligence analysis of weapons' effectiveness in the guerrilla war. . . . attempts to thin out the trees in jungle refuges have scarcely affected Communist military operations so far, the analysis found. Even inexperienced guerrillas have learned to protect themselves from aerial cannon and rocket bombardment. . . .
>
> The Vietcong are known to have taken elaborate precaution against attack. Their main base areas consist largely of underground tunnels and caves, strong enough in some cases to withstand direct hits from 500-pound bombs.
>
> Guerrilla veterans have learned to spot various types of aircraft and estimate whether their mission is bombardment, defoliation, reconnaissance or transport.
>
> The intelligence analysis shows that some Vietcong units have specially trained persons who count falling bombs or incoming artillery shells and correlate them with the explosions heard. This way they try to detect duds, which they can collect for their own use [for land mines, bombs, grenades, etc.].

The ratio of government casualties to Viet Cong casualties sharply altered with the passage of time, the former increasing and the latter decreasing, even by the government's own estimates. Official figures as reported by *The New York Times* of October 18, 1964, show:

1961—Government casualties, 9,000; Viet Cong, 13,000.
1962—Government, 13,000; Viet Cong, 33,000.
1963—Government, 19,000; Viet Cong, 28,000.
1964—First six months: Government, 11,390; Viet Cong 9,000.

It is well to bear in mind that the casualties of the Viet Cong reported by Saigon (1) are estimates, made by the other side, and (2) almost inevitably include civilian victims of aerial bombing and artillery attacks, conveniently assumed to be Viet Cong rather than positively identified as such. One test is to compare the number of weapons captured by the government with the number of Viet Cong casualties reported, as against government casualties reported and weapons *lost.* In the latter instance, there is a general correspondence; in the former, a surprising disparity. The arms captured from the Viet Cong rarely if ever match the reported Viet Cong casualty lists, a fact that raises the strong suspicion that the dead in question were not armed in the first place.

Again, the high proportion of reported enemy casualties arising from air operations raises a question about the accuracy of the casualty reports. Who, in fact, counts the bodies, much less identifies them as those of combatants?

In this connection, Bernard Fall writes in *The Two Viet-Nams:*

How the tactical aircraft now in Viet-Nam are used can be discerned from the official reports of the South Vietnamese Air Force. In a not untypical three-day operation in January, 1963, the VNAF hit the following targets: 1 house and 20 watchtowers 10 and 22 miles west of Pleiku; 3 houses 28 miles west of Qui-Nhon; 4 houses and a rice field 22 miles west of Pleiku; 25 houses destroyed and 10 damaged 17 miles southwest of Quang-Ngai; 15 houses 22 miles northwest of Pleiku; 2 houses 19 miles north of Bien-Hoa. And in operations against Viet-Cong concentrations in the Plain of Reeds and the jungle bastion of Zone D north of Saigon, the ARVN [Army of the Republic of Viet Nam] reported 76 enemy killed by ground fire, 400 killed by aerial gunnery, but only 9 individual weapons and 5 crew-served weapons (machine guns, mortars) captured—and "over 400 houses and huts destroyed."

It takes little imagination to guess who the "enemy" casualties must be in such circumstances.

The indiscriminate use of aircraft against presumed Viet Cong targets does much to explain the alienation of the rural population from the Saigon government. Country people whose only contact with the government comes in the form of napalm and rocket attacks can scarcely be expected to feel sympathetic to the government cause, whatever it may be. On the other hand, they have every reason to feel solidarity with the guerrillas, usually recruited from their own villages, who share their peril and their hardships.

To the world outside South Vietnam's hamlets and villages, the insurgents are agents of international Communism. In the grass and bamboo huts where they live, in the hamlets they have "liberated," the Vietcong guerrillas talk like local people about simple things.

"It was hell when we were attacked every night in my hamlet," said a peasant's son in his early 20's. "If the Government was good enough or strong enough, I thought it should have been able to protect us at night. So I thought maybe the Liberation Front people were right," he said. "Now I know they are. I don't regret my decision to join them."

Another young man said: "I was scared and angry when they attacked our hamlet. But I had to go along with them, and now I'm glad I did."

The questioner was a Vietnamese reporter. He had taken local buses to hamlets in insecure or disputed areas in the delta and found himself in a hamlet about which there was no dispute. Night and day it was governed by the Communists. . . . Except for the leader, the guerrillas seemed to be in their late teens or early 20's. They would not give their names, for fear of disclosure to the Government. They all said they were natives of the hamlet. All spoke Vietnamese with the local accent. . . .

Asked what they think about Ho Chi Minh, President of North Vietnam, the leader said: "He is a great revolutionary. We like

him but do not take orders from him. We are South Vietnamese
and are fighting for the liberation of South Vietnam."
                        —*The New York Times*, November 23, 1964.

In the greater part of rural South Viet Nam, the Viet Cong
administers the only government that exists, operating its own
schools and hospitals, its own census, farm bureaus, tax agen-
cies, news agency. Increasingly, it rules by default—because
there is no effective government agency present, the only contact
with Saigon being the occasional punitive expeditions of the
armed forces, ferried in by helicopter or risking the heavily
mined roads in armored motor columns. When the army leaves,
as it must, life goes on as before, and gradually, through incessant pressure on army outposts and government installations in
twilight areas, the Viet Cong extends its domain.

Lip service is paid in Washington and Saigon to the idea that
the crux of the struggle is popular support, without which the
war cannot be won. "We must keep in mind," said Lieutenant
General William C. Westmoreland, on assuming command of
the United States task force in South Viet Nam, "that campaigns
must be won at province, district, village and hamlet levels,
where battle is being waged for the hearts and minds of the
people."

So far, the means of attaining this laudable objective have not
been discovered. Napalm fire-bombs and chemical sprays that
defoliate the crops along with the jungle do not seem to win
hearts or minds.

In 1962, the Ngo regime began a program modeled on British
practice in Malaya to move the rural population into so-called
strategic hamlets—a $60 million effort involving the construc-
tion of thousands of fortified stockade communities and the destruction of scattered dwellings—as the means of cutting the
insurgency off from its popular base.

The announced objective was 12,000 fortified hamlets by the
end of 1963, sufficient to house virtually the entire rural population of South Viet Nam. The number actually built remained in
doubt because of false reports from government officials in
charge of the program—and because many of the fortified ham-

lets fell into Viet Cong hands or were destroyed almost as soon as they were completed. By early 1964 the program had bogged down to such an extent that the Associated Press reported:

> The Diem regime was cast into oblivion four months ago but Americans in Vietnam still see no noticeable improvement in the general policy governing the strategic hamlets. Most Americans with anything to do with the $60 million program that began with a blaze of publicity 2 years ago say it continues to deteriorate.

The forcible removal of villagers from their old dwellings, inadequate compensation for losses involved in the transfer, and the concentration-camp character of the stockade hamlets with their barbed wire and concrete pill boxes, had the opposite effect of that intended. Instead of winning the confidence of the villagers, the program further alienated them. Rather than be forced into the hamlets, young men vanished into the forest to join the Viet Cong, and the younger women were quick to follow them, leaving many of the new communities populated almost exclusively by dependents—the very young and the very old.

\* \* \*

Plans to rebuild the national police force were considered an important part of the counterinsurgency program, and eleven police institutes were established in various parts of the country, with the object of raising police strength to 50,000 by the end of 1965. The police were considered a crucial element in the process of holding areas once cleared of Viet Cong guerrillas—to check on all movements within the country, to ferret out suspected Viet Cong agents, and to maintain law and order in the villages, where the official links with the central government have broken down.

The program appeared plausible on the face of it, but the question remained: How would the police themselves be secure, where even military patrols were not?

Even the fortified hamlets, with strong local militia forces, were subject to guerrilla attack, and often they were attacked precisely because of the military booty they offered—weapons, radio transmitters, medicines, provisions. Logically the same would apply to any police posts that might be established. Police are confronted by the same dilemma as the military: If concentrated in strong points they fail in their purpose, which is to occupy and govern the rural countryside; yet if they are scattered through the villages, they will be too few—even 50,000 strong—to defend themselves, and can be eliminated a single unit at a time.

The situation recalls General Giap's pronouncement: "This war can have only one objective—the occupation and subjection of the country. The nature and the very aim of the campaign he is conducting oblige the enemy to split up his forces so as to be able to occupy the invaded territory. During the war against the French . . . the enemy was thus faced with a contradiction: It was impossible for him to occupy the invaded territory without dividing his forces. By their dispersal, he created difficulties for himself. His scattered units thus became an easy prey for our troops and mobile forces dwindled more and more. . . ."

\*   \*   \*

Giap's statement is more than an analysis. In the critical spring of 1965, it could have been taken as a warning. To expand the war, to commit sufficient American troops to cope with the exasperating war of the flea in Viet Nam—this was an understandable temptation for American military men thinking in terms of military problems and narrow objectives, thinking to stand above politics and to concern themselves only with the outcome of battles.

But even in the narrowest military context, could an American expeditionary force conquer Viet Nam, where a French expeditionary force had failed?

The French, at least, did not believe so, on the basis of their own hard experience.

"It does not appear," President De Gaulle told a new conference in Paris on July 23, 1964, "that there can be a military solution in South Vietnam. It is true that certain people imagine that the Americans could seek elsewhere this military solution that they could not find on the spot, by extending the war to the North as far as was necessary, and surely they have all the means for this.

"But it is rather difficult to accept that they could wish to assume the enormous risk of a general war. Then, since war cannot bring a solution, one must make peace. This implies a return to the agreement made ten years ago. . . ."

To return to the conditions of a decade ago would be to return to the terms of a treaty—binding on Ho Chi Minh and his government but not clearly binding on the South Vietnamese insurgents—by which the French accepted defeat after a war that had cost them five billions of dollars and 172,000 dead, wounded, and missing, a struggle in which the Vietminh, too, had paid dearly for the independence of the North, with some 300,000 casualties.

It seemed highly unlikely that the Viet Cong could be persuaded to accept, in 1965, after another decade of sacrifice, a return to the conditions of 1954. Why should they?

On the other hand, there was little doubt that they would be inclined to accept a political victory that they had not yet been able to achieve by military means.

As U.S. Deputy Ambassador U. Alexis Johnson summed up the outlook for a negotiated peace in an interview with *Life*, in November, 1964:

"Their present strategy is designed toward bringing about negotiations between some government in Saigon and their political arm, which is the National Liberation Front. This negotiation would be directed toward formation of a coalition government. The second step would be for the NLF to take over that government. And the third step would be integration with North Vietnam."

Such a solution had already been ruled out in Washington, but—in a military stalemate—political pressures in Saigon could easily reach the explosion point at which a popular decision could override American policy, and sweep away any government that supported it.

Meanwhile, the war of the flea continued, a war now of plague proportions. The flea can endure: his war is fought in space and time, and each passing day raises the third factor of protracted, revolutionary war—the *will* of the people to resist. Since their opponent could not say the same, the outcome— barring an extension of the struggle that might become general war—seemed to be a foregone conclusion.

The record stands: No colonial war has yet been lost by a colonial people, once entered into.

# WARS OF NATIONAL LIBERATION AND THEIR COST. THE IRISH "TROUBLES" AND THE ROLE OF THE BLACK AND TANS. TERRORISM IN ISRAEL. REBELLION IN NORTH AFRICA.

The price of national liberation can come high, as the toll of the two wars in Viet Nam bears witness. Yet in general it can be said that modern wars of national liberation—those of the remaining colonies and those of the semi-colonies, such as Cuba—have been remarkably economical of human life, as compared with wars between equal states and alliances of states.

Actual battle casualties in Cuba, for example, cannot have exceeded a few hundred killed during two years of civil strife.

Revolutionary sources, immediately after Batista's fall, claimed some 20,000 dead as the seven-year toll of police terror under the dictatorship. No listing or other attempt at verification has ever been published, nor have battle casualties ever been totalled. Accounts of individual battles by Guevara and others, however, indicate a very modest final figure.

In Zanzibar recently, the toll probably was closer to a few dozen. In Cyprus, it did not go over three figures. The same is true for Israel, if one counts only the period of hostilities between the Jews and the British, and not the Arab-Israeli war that followed. In Ireland, writes Richard Bennett:

> The I.R.A., in its first year of war against England, had killed at most twenty-six people, eighteen of them policemen, and had

fired shots in anger at human targets . . . on not much more than a hundred occasions.*

"No government," adds Bennett, "could capitulate to such a threat." He is wrong. The fact is that England *did* capitulate, if not to the threat *per se,* then to the intolerable political and economic situation that it was to produce, given another year.

Here is yet another illustration of the nature of the war of the flea, of which guerrilla tactics is one aspect and *terrorism* (urban guerrilla-ism) is another.

Bombs and bullets are the physical weapons of the rural guerrilla and equally of the urban terrorist, but the real lever for both is politics. Divisions may be destroyed, as in Viet Nam, but this is not the ultimate objective; cities may be terrorized, as in Cyprus, but again this is not the goal. The purpose of the war of national liberation, pitting the feeble resources of a small and primitive nation against the strength of a great, industrial power is not to conquer or to terrorize, but to *create an intolerable situation for the occupying power or its puppet government.*

In the war of the flea, parliamentary cannonades wreak more havoc than artillery; headlines burst bigger than bombs; peace marches win battles where machine guns fail. Casualties are low because guerrillas, while fighting *campaigns* of attrition, shun the *battles* of attrition common to regular armies. Terrorism, conventionally viewed with pious horror as political murder (but how more murderous than blockbusting a city or napalming a village?) is far more humane, being more selective, than most other types of warfare.

In the end, the oppressive power relinquishes its grasp not because its armies have been defeated in battle (although, as we have seen, this may occur), but because the satellite, the rebellious colony, through terrorism and guerrilla warfare, becomes (1) too great a political embarrassment to be sustained domestically or on the world stage, (2) unprofitable, too expensive, or no longer prestigious.

*The Black and Tans; Houghton Mifflin Co., Boston.

The rebel casts himself in the role of David, and makes it his business to force the enemy into the role of Goliath in the public mind. His every act and announcement play on the sympathies and sense of justice of the global witnesses of the struggle, by creating the picture of a courageous people fighting for independence against the monstrous forces of tyranny and oppression.

At the same time, the entire arsenal of revolution—guerrilla fighting, terror, sabotage, propaganda—is brought to bear in an effort to take the profit out of colonialism by demoralizing labor and impeding production, boycotting imports, inciting insurrection, forbidding payment of rents to foreign owners, wrecking foreign industrial installations, and in every way increasing the *cost* of exploitation and of political control—the expense of maintaining the bureaucracy and the police and military forces that must be used to put down the rebellion.

If the goal is clearly understood and revolutionary tactics are resolutely applied, the colonial power quickly becomes involved in a struggle that simultaneously blackens it before the world and inflicts financial losses that will soon be translated, at home, into political liabilities. The very efforts of a colonial power to end the struggle will only accelerate the process, for the more stringent the methods of suppression applied, the greater the hatred of the colonial population for the colonizers (or of the satellite people for the imperialists), and the harsher the picture of oppression to be held up before the world.

Note: the *world* includes the population of the oppressor nation, and, more particularly, the government's domestic political opposition, which will be sure to raise a hue and cry about the methods used to put down the rebellion, as well as the burden on the taxpayers, the loss of national prestige, et cetera, et cetera.

Excellent examples of this entire process may be drawn from the experience of the two great empire builders of the last century, Britain and France. For the former, the struggle that led to the (still conditional) independence of Cyprus was almost blow for blow a repetition of "the troubles" that had freed Catholic Ireland from the English rule more than three decades earlier. The lessons of Ireland were also applied in Israel; leaders of the Irgun and the Stern Group studied the writings of the Irish Republican Army commanders, the better to know their enemy and the means by which he could be driven out of Palestine or, if not driven out, forced to end a situation that terror made politically and financially intolerable.

The purpose of terror, said Lenin, is to terrify. He might have strengthened the observation, while weakening the aphorism, by remarking that its greater purpose is to sabotage the orderly administration of government by forcing those who govern into a defensive position in which nothing can be accomplished without the continual, crippling presence of an armed guard. Its secondary effect, if not its purpose, is to induce a *counterterrorism* that serves the rebel cause better than any stratagem the rebels themselves could devise.

This was the case in Ireland, where, despite a long history of insurrection, public support of the independence movement was lukewarm until fired by the acts of the British themselves—in particular by the depredations of the notorious "Black and Tans," recruited to strengthen the Royal Irish Constabulary.

Of the ill-starred Easter Rebellion raised by Irish nationalists in 1916, four years before the Tans were heard of, Richard Bennett writes in *The Black and Tans:*

> The Easter Rebellion was a sadly mismanaged enterprise. The rebels proclaimed the Republic, occupied a number of buildings in Dublin and held out bravely for a week. A young mathematics teacher called de Valera was the last to surrender. There was little trouble in the rest of Ireland. The Irish people declined the nobly worded invitation 'to prove itself worthy of the august destiny to which it is called,' and looting Dubliners made hay while the shells crashed and the bullets flew.
>
> Never in the history of Ireland had a rebellion inspired so little sympathy. There were nearly a hundred thousand Catholic Irishmen fighting with the British Army, and the rebellion seemed as much a stab in the back to the majority of Irish people as it did to the English. The prisoners, who were marched through the streets, passed between lines of angry, jeering Dubliners. The cause of Irish independence seemed lost, or postponed to some far-distant date.

At this point, the British made a fatal mistake. They proceeded to shoot fifteen leaders of the Easter Rebellion. The executions caused a scandal that spread around the world, and ended any hope of a peaceful solution of the Irish question. The fortunes of the almost discredited Sinn Fein independence movement, provided with a set of holy martyrs, quickly revived. But London went ahead, almost as if deliberately inviting its own defeat, by preparing a conscription act—the Great War in Europe was then in progress and manpower was desperately needed—to draft Irishmen of military age. The measure united the country against the Crown and sent thousands of young men into the Irish militia known as the National Volunteers, soon to be converted into the revolutionary Irish Republican Army. England could not have done more to set the stage for "the troubles" to come.

On January 21, 1919, the Dail Eireann, the legislative assembly of the Sinn Fein party, declared its independence from Britain and proceeded to constitute itself a *de facto* republican government on Irish soil, soon to be complete even to Sinn Fein courts and police. The maneuver was political in intent; actual war was not envisioned. Yet the intention of the Dail was one thing and the temper of the Volunteers another. Scarcely had the declaration of independence been signed when the first shots of the revolution were fired. On the very same day a group of Volunteers ambushed a party transporting gelignite to a query and killed two members of the Royal Irish Constabulary.

Scattered, more or less spontaneous clashes between police and Volunteers soon gave way to an organized campaign of raids and ambushes, under the direction of Michael Collins in Dublin and of I.R.A. brigade commanders elsewhere. Actual casualties were relatively few, but the effects were remarkable. Helmeted soldiers patrolled the streets of Dublin with fixed bayonets as in a foreign capital under wartime occupation; the docks were piled high with war materiel, and every delivery of arms or military supplies moving over the roads required an escort of armored cars and tenders filled with troops, for fear of the I.R.A. Hundreds of political prisoners crowded the jails, and the Crown forces were kept so busy with searches for arms and

I.R.A. suspects that more than 20,000 house raids were recorded between January of 1919 and March, 1920.

By the end of 1919 a bitter struggle was in progress that exempted no one, military or civilian. The country had become an armed camp in which assassinations and raids on military barracks were daily occurrences. In Dublin the atmosphere was such that "nearly every important British official connected with the Dublin Castle Administration was virtually interned in the Castle," and, "conditions for the soldiers and police in their barracks were not much better. There was little action, but there was no lull in the atmosphere of suspense. Any road might lead to an ambush; the most harmless-looking civilian might suddenly draw a gun and fire."

Scarcely a day passed that failed to provide its headline-making "Irish incident" for the avid British press. Abroad, thanks to Eamon de Valera's highly effective propaganda campaign among the Irish immigrants in America, sympathy for the rebel cause reached such dimensions that the British envoy to Washington reported himself to be "almost powerless for good owing to the universal sentiment in favour of Ireland."

Forty-three thousand British troops occupied Ireland, in addition to the 10,000-man Royal Irish Constabulary, soon to be augmented by several thousand Black and Tans, whose nickname derived from their mixed uniform of military khakis and R.I.C. black Sam Browne belts, holsters, boots, and cap visors; these later were joined by some 1,500 "temporary cadets" of the R.I.C. Auxiliary. For controlling the 26,000 square miles of insurgent southern Ireland, it was scarcely sufficient.

The terrain was ideal for guerrilla fighting—the green, rugged, and in many places virtually roadless countryside being impassable to motor transport during wet weather, which seemed to be most of the time. I.R.A. men "on the run," as the Irish expression had it, found perfect sanctuary in the bogs and wooded mountains, yet were always close enough to towns and main arteries to launch lightning raids under cover of darkness and quickly withdraw. In the cities, the gunmen of the I.R.A. were so well integrated with the populace at large that most of them held regular civilian employment, and the majority of

I.R.A. operations in Dublin and Cork were scheduled at night for that reason: there was insufficient manpower available during daylight hours.

The I.R.A. action consisted for the greater part of arms raids on military barracks, ambushes of military convoys in the countryside, and attacks on small patrols or individual R.I.C. men and soldiers in the cities. In addition, there was a "special squad" in Dublin that specialized in the assassination of British intelligence agents and political figures.

From the military point of view, much of this activity had only nuisance value. Newspaper ink flowed more freely than blood. I.R.A. gunmen missed more often than hit their targets. The barracks that burned were often empty and their destruction only symbolic; often, too, the raiders were repulsed, having expended more ammunition than they had hoped to capture, and the victims of the gunmen were more frequently Irish than English—suspected informers, collaborators, and the like.

The I.R.A. was not, however, fighting a military war; it was fighting a political war, and the true effects of the terror were psychological and political. Enlistments in the R.I.C. stopped and resignations mounted as morale sagged. The troops in their quarters—foreigners in a hostile country—lived under a strain which veterans of the war in Europe said was greater than that of the trenches. At one point, the fear of the I.R.A. gunmen—and any casual stroller might be a gunman—reached such intensity that a military order was posted warning civilians that any man walking with his hands in his pockets was liable to be shot on sight. Pockets could conceal pistols, and the British were taking no chances.

The raids on barracks and convoys may have been ineffective militarily, but they had their effect on the economy and the orderly administration of a country being systematically plunged into chaos. The mere chance of a raid or an ambush, anywhere, at any time, slowed transport, restricted production, and forced the military to stay constantly on the alert—to guard all barracks, all convoys, all public buildings, to travel only in strength, to continually screen civilians, check credentials, search buildings, to interfere with traffic and with all of the multifarious activities of everyday life—at tremendous cost to the government, to the war-weary British taxpayer, to the straitened British owner of Irish properties, to investors, the banks, and all who had a stake in an orderly, productive Ireland. Each incident was another damaging blow to British prestige abroad, each shook British morale at home, and each was sure to be seized upon by the Labour Party and the Liberals as fresh ammunition to be hurled at the Conservative government. If the military could stand the strain, Downing Street could not.

Predictably, efforts to control the situation only worsened it. The Black and Tans, arriving early in 1920, were a godsend to the I.R.A. For every incident the latter produced, the former produced another, and where the actions of the I.R.A. could be admired abroad, as part of a courageous struggle for liberty, the reprisals of the Tans could only draw blame—and further unite the Irish in opposition to the Crown.

Irish propagandists made the most of oppression, so that the burning of a few shops and homes became magnified into the rape of entire villages, and the summary execution of a relative handful of Sinn Feiners or suspected I.R.A. men became indiscriminate slaughter on a major scale. When a divisional commander of the R.I.C. told his men to "shoot first, ask questions later," the clandestine *Irish Bulletin* quoted him as having said:

> If a police barracks is burned or if the barracks already occupied is not suitable, then the best house in the locality is to be commandeered, the occupants thrown into the gutter. Let them die there—the more the merrier. Police and military will patrol the country at least five nights a week. They are not to confine themselves to the main roads, but make across the country, lie in ambush, and, when civilians are seen approaching, shout "Hands up!" Should the order be not immediately obeyed, shoot and shoot with effect. If persons approaching carry their hands in their pockets, or are in any way suspicious-looking, shoot them down.
>
> You may make mistakes occasionally and innocent persons may be shot, but that cannot be helped, and you are bound to get the right parties some time. The more you shoot, the better I will

like you, and I assure you no policeman will get into trouble for shooting any man. . . .*

The report was duly denied, but it made little difference. It might as well have been true: There was sufficient truth in it to make it credible, and that was what counted. It was all of a piece with accounts that told of lorry loads of Black and Tans roaring through village streets "firing their rifles at random to the peril of anyone who happened to be in the way," and singing:

> "We are the boys of the R.I.C.
> As happy as happy can be."

Whether the Tans actually sang such a ditty on their forays is of little importance. What was important was the reputation they created for themselves, and the effects of it. Singing or not singing, they did sufficient irresponsible killing, burning, dynamiting of houses, and drunken pillaging to create a scandal in England, and the scandal aided the Irish cause. The *Daily News* of London virtually accused the government of "secretly conniving at the barbarous reprisals now being systematically carried out;" and the conservative *Times* declared: "Day by day the tidings from Ireland grow worse. The accounts of arson and destruction . . . must fill English readers with a sense of shame. . . . The name of England is being sullied throughout the Empire and throughout the world by this savagery for which the Government can no longer escape, however much they may seek to disclaim responsibility."

Where the counterterrorism of the Tans and the Auxiliaries shocked the British public, the martyrdom of various Irish heroes—Terence MacSwiney, Lord Mayor of Cork, who died in Brixton Gaol after a hunger strike lasting seventy days; young Kevin Barry, hanged in Dublin for killing a British soldier—captured the sympathy of millions of loyal Britons.

The I.R.A. never gained sufficient strength to defeat the British military forces in any engagement of any size anywhere at

*Quoted in *The Black and Tans*.

any time. Although the British Viceroy, Lord French, estimated it as some 100,000 strong and the British Secretary for Ireland doubled the estimate, reporting an army of 200,000, "ready to murder by day and night," its peak strength, on paper, was never more than 15,000 men, and Michael Collins later put the effective fighting strength of the I.R.A. at 3,000.

But then, as noted before, the Irish rebellion was a political rather than a military contest, and the truce that ended it late in 1921 brought a political victory that obviated the need of a military decision. For political victory, three thousand armed men were enough. Their role was more that of catalyst than agent. Their militancy had accomplished two things: It had transformed an apathetic population into one actively hostile to British rule, so creating a massive resistance that the English could not economically or—in terms of politics—practically overcome; and it had induced a counterterrorism which, again for political reasons, defeated its own purpose. If at the end of some centuries of sporadic struggle against foreign domination the Irish failed to hurl the English invader into the sea, they accomplished something better and more economical: By their resistance they took the profit out of colonialism and turned the colony from a British asset into a liability, so, in effect, *persuading* the enemy to withdraw.

There was nothing very novel about the means employed by the terrorists; they were such as ordinary ingenuity might suggest. Fires were set in public buildings. Irish flags were flown with grenades attached to the lanyards to booby-trap the soldiers who came to remove them. Slates were removed from the roofs of police stations and gasoline was poured into the attics, to be set afire. Bridges were blown up and rails removed from railroad tracks. Sugar was put into gasoline tanks, sand in crankcases, emery dust in machinery gears.

The means of sabotage and of armed aggression were simple, and the actual damage relatively unimportant. What was important was (1) the cost of suppressing such a campaign and (2) its political effects on both the Irish and the English people, the one being unified and forced into an active involvement, the other divided and rendered impotent by the same effort—and its consequences.

* * *

Could the British have won in Ireland by putting a huge army into the field and waging a Cromwellian war of extermination to suppress the rebellion? In the twentieth century, the question is meaningless. British public opinion—related always to economic considerations—would not have permitted such a solution, even had it been considered. A generation later, world opinion forebade any similar approach to the problem of Palestine, the problem of Cyprus, the problem, for that matter, of Suez, where the abortive Anglo-French invasion of 1956 produced global repercussions.

Draconian solutions are possible only in isolation, in an indifferent world, and even then, only against a population that has not the will to resist.

In Palestine, for example, the British were able to wage a vigorous campaign against the so-called dissident political factions, the Irgun Zvai Leumi and the smaller Lohmey Heruth Israel (Lehi) or Stern Group, only for so long as the Jewish Agency and other conservative Jewish elements in Palestine and abroad turned their faces against violence. The stiffening of Jewish resistance in reaction to the suppression campaign and to continued British restrictions on immigration, and at last the entrance of the Haganah into the struggle in 1945 confronted the British with a choice that was no choice—they could declare war on the entire Jewish nation, or surrender the Palestine mandate. They wisely chose to surrender the mandate and leave the question of the future Jewish state to the United Nations.

Contemporary historians, even Jewish historians, have tended to deprecate the role of the Irgun and even more that of the Sternists in the struggle for Israeli independence. Yet it seems clear that their contribution was vital: It was to create an open struggle without which there could have been no resolution of the issues, without which the British withdrawl might have been postponed indefinitely. The terrorists had no illusions about their ability to free Israel by their own efforts: Irgun numbered no more than two thousand fighting men; Lehi never had more than four hundred. Their purpose, rather, was to demonstrate to the British the immense cost in money and manpower of continuing to rule in the face of determined Jewish resistance, and to arouse the Jewish people until all Jews were united in opposition to the foreigner.

Lacking weapons and manpower and the capacity for important sabotage or large-scale guerrilla warfare, Lehi chose the tactics most suitable to its means: individual terrorism. On November 6, 1944, the campaign reached out to Cairo, to strike down Lord Moyne, British Minister of State in the Middle East. *The Deed*, as Gerold Frank called it in his illuminating study of the assassination, shocked the British and horrified conservative Jewry everywhere. The two young terrorists who had killed Lord Moyne, subsequently hanged for their act, were universally reviled. As Frank relates:

> The Hebrew press could not find words strong enough to denounce the deed. It was an "abomination. . . ." "Since Zionism began," lamented *Haaretz*, the most influential newspaper in the country, "no more grievous blow has been struck at our cause." The Jewish Agency expressed its horror "at this revolting crime." In London Dr. Chaim Weizmann . . . said this shock had been "far more severe and numbing than that of the death of my own son."*

A shock, certainly; but that had been the intention, and those who feared for the cause of Israeli independence were mistaken. By the end of another year, the quickening cycle of violence and repression had created sufficient shocks to arouse the Jewish people, and to convince the British that they were engaged in a hopeless task, a contest that they could not hope to win but only to prolong and intensify.

As Gerold Frank writes in *The Deed*:

> Certainly the independence for which the two [terrorists] were hanged in 1945 would not have been won in 1948 without dec-

*The Deed*, by Gerold Frank; Simon and Schuster, Inc., New York; 1963.

ades of political activity in England, in Europe, in the United States, in Palestine and elsewhere; without the immigration and colonization and labors of hundreds of thousands; without, in the end, a determined citizenry, a resourceful army and an indomitable leadership. Nor, without all these, would that independence have been maintained in the years that followed.

But there is no doubt that the deed was one of the great irritations, the great harassments, which so annoyed and confused and bedeviled the British that ultimately they gave the problem over to the United Nations—and thus opened the door to the partition of Palestine and the first Jewish state in two thousand years.*

There is a point to be made here. If revolution is to be understood as a historical, social process, rather than an accident or a plot, then it will not do to consider guerrillas, terrorists, political assassins as deviants or agents somehow apart from the social fabric, irrelevant or only fortuitously relevant to the historical process. Guerrillas are *of* the people, or they cannot survive, cannot even come into being. Terrorism, while it arouses the popular will to revolt, is at the same time a manifestation of that will, expressing the first stiffening of popular resistance to established authority, the first surge of the popular impulse toward a new and different order of existence. It may be argued that terroristic movements attract criminals and psychopaths. So they do. But criminality itself is a form of unconscious social protest, reflecting the distortions of an imperfect society, and in a revolutionary situation the criminal, the psychopath, may become as good a revolutionary as the idealist.

In Palestine, those who directed the terror were not adventurers, but a vanguard. In their actions, they expressed the long-suppressed fury and frustration of a hundred generations of oppressed and spat-upon Jewry. More especially they acted for the living generation, witnesses to the final racial catastrophe, the Hitlerian blood bath in Europe, whose shattered survivors were now—ultimate insult—forbidden refuge in the land of their ancestors. The seething spirit of the terror in Palestine was vividly voiced in an almost biblical warning to the British published in

*Ibid.*

June, 1944, in the Lehi organ *Hazit,* after a young member of the organization had been sentenced to hang for shooting at a policeman:

> This is how you British will walk the streets of Zion from now on: armed to the teeth, prepared for anything and fear in your eyes: fear from every dark corner, in every turn in the road, every sound at night, fear from every Jewish boy, fear day and night because the Jewish youth have become dynamite in this country. You shall walk on burning embers, our bodies will be the embers and our love of country the fire. No guards, no tanks, no fines, no curfews, no tortures and no hangings, no prisons and no detention camps, will help your High Commissioners, your officers, your policemen. We are fed up, we tell you. Your children will become orphans just as you orphaned the Children of Israel. Your mothers will lose their sons just as you made the mothers of Israel mourn for their sons. For every cry of a boy from the top of a burning boat, for every cry of a Hebrew mother when her child embarks on a broken ship in the middle of the sea, for every Jewish tear that is unanswered—we shall answer you. We came in fire and we were burned: we came in water and we were drowned: we the remnants walk in rivers of blood, the blood reaches our necks, our mouths, our eyes, and from the fire and water and blood, trembling arms are raised, voices cry out, and from the mouths and eyes and from the trembling arms and fingers, from the water and the fire and blood, from there we are coming up, we are coming. Woe unto you! [Quoted by Gerold Frank in *The Deed.*]

Here is the voice of a people, speaking with the awesome moral authority conferred by the reeking charnel houses of Europe, where six million Jews were dying or dead. Reckless the ruler who would defy it!

The British were committed, tied to a policy of Arab appeasement by the petroleum pipelines of the Middle East, conscience drowned in a sea of oil—but they were not insane. They could not, before the eyes of the world, go on hanging Jews. They got out.

\* \* \*

Revolution comes in various ways. It came to French Morocco as a *jehad*, a holy war, brought on by the banishment of the independent-minded sultan, Mohammad ben Youssef, and the substitution of a puppet, the aged ben Arafa, on the throne in Rabat. Corpses found at dawn in the streets of Casablanca were often those of Moslems who had touched alcohol, forbidden by Islam and especially sacrilegious during a time of mourning for the true sultan, in exile on the island of Madagascar. When smoke arose from the *medinas,* it was invariably a burning tobacco shop: tobacco was forbidden by the same religious austerity and boycotted as a French government monopoly. When a lamb was sacrificed in the courtyard of the sultan's palace, only the shameless attended. Ramadan, the holy month, was not observed by the faithful—another symbol of mourning and protest. Houses went unpainted. Frivolity and ostentation were punished by the swift knives of the Istiqlal, the People's Party.

For the rest, the resistance that was to end the French protectorate and restore Moroccan independence followed a familiar pattern. Exploding bombs, sabotage, and the assassination of Moslem collaborators—native policemen, postmen, *caids* subservient to the French—aroused the passions of the people and involved them in continual conflict with the colonial authorities. Demonstrations in the native quarters grew into riots that overflowed the walls of the *medinas.* One after the other, from city to city, they swept Morocco during the hot summer of 1955, and in each the French made the same mistake, panicky police opening fire on unruly crowds, killing a dozen here, a score there, thirty in another place, as the insurrection spread from Casablanca to Marrakesh, Meknes, Fez, Rabat.

Across the country, agitators of the Istiqlal incited the primitive Bedouin hill tribes with tales of impending liberation. Tribesmen swooping down on the highway town of Oued Zem, in the broiling Tadla Plain, massacred two hundred Europeans, sacked a nearby mining community. There were uprisings in the Middle Atlas, ambushes on the roads; eight foreign correspondents were killed on a single day in August. Rioters in Casablanca and Istiqlal snipers firing from the rooftops threw the city into a state of siege. The persistent cry of the rioters was, ''Restore ben Youssef!" But the restoration was only a symbolic objective: Ben Youssef meant independence, and holy war against the French who withheld it.

Terrorism was more effective than guerrilla tactics in Morocco. A true guerrilla campaign never developed, although a few hundred raiders from Spanish Morocco began such a campaign—and tied up a division of Foreign Legionnaires and Spahis in the mountains of the Riff for some weeks during the autumn of 1955.

The struggle ended in the capitulation of the French government, through a series of compromises: the announcement that the Sultan ben Youssef would be permitted to leave his exile in Madagascar for Paris created jubilant demonstrations in Morocco that forced a greater concession: he would return to Rabat. The departure of the aged pretender, ben Arafa, set off new demonstrations. The actual return of the Sultan brought the entire Moslem population into the streets, and the fifty-year-old protectorate became a hollow pretense which Paris hastily abandoned.

The formula followed by the Istiqlal was simple enough: terror and sabotage served the twofold purpose of taking the profit out of colonialism and making the country unsafe for the colonists. The terrorists could not be controlled except by throwing the country into a state of siege, and the psychological effect of the siege, with its curfews, arrests, searches, and massive military movements, was to bring the Moslem population into the conflict in riotous demonstrations which no army could suppress. Since a colony that cannot be controlled is of no value and of great expense, the purpose of occupying it as a colony ceased to exist, and Paris—under political pressure at home—wisely accepted a settlement with an essentially conservative independence movement that preserved major French interests in the country.

The victory cannot be called bloodless. Scores died in rioting and several hundred were massacred in local uprisings as the end approached. Terrorism took a heavier toll of Moroccan collaborators than of the French, by far. *Ratissages* by French troops and the Foreign Legion claimed an unknown number of victims:

In the wake of the Oued Zem massacre, the French were said to have killed twenty thousand Moslems in and around the Tadla Plain. The figure was supplied by the Istiqlal and is no doubt exaggerated, but it is established beyond question that villages were bombed and strafed; jet fighters and bombers were sent into action and the roads rumbled with tanks and weapons carriers for weeks after the Oued Zem incident. In Oued Zem itself, Spahis used artillery to level the native quarter where raiding Bedouins had taken refuge when the first troops had arrived, and heavy tanks rolled over the rubble to make certain there would be no survivors.*

The ultimate cost was nevertheless far lighter than it might have been, the terror more merciful (if that is the word) than any campaign of what we choose to call *conventional* war.

The reason is clear. In Morocco, as in Israel and Ireland, revolutionary warfare provided a shortcut; the pressures generated by terrorism and political agitation proved more potent than infantry divisions and aircraft.

In Tunisia a similar solution had been reached. Algeria is another case; it is one that deserves and requires far more space than is available here to recount it. The North African territory had long been regarded as an integral part of France, not merely a colony. It had been settled by the French more than a century earlier, virtually *created* by the French, and a million French *colons* considered it their native land.

France, still bleeding from the wounds to pride and pocket inflicted in Indochina, could not without a serious struggle relinquish its grasp on its last-remaining major overseas possession, and so it is not surprising that a major struggle ensued.

Urban terrorism, although important, was far from decisive in Algeria, where too much was at stake for the French to permit

---

*My wife and I were on the scene as news correspondents on the night of the massacre, while the fighting was still in progress and the burned bodies of the victims still lay in the streets. A Spahi captain who took part in the subsequent mopping up operation told me later about the use to which the artillery and tanks were put after the town had been closed to newsmen and we had returned to Casablanca.—Author.

themselves to be blackmailed into compromise. Full-scale guerrilla warfare began with seventy simultaneous attacks across the
country on October 31, 1954, launched more for their psychological effect than for practical military reasons. The principal
stronghold of the rebellion was the rugged Aurès mountain region, where, as Michael K. Clark has noted in *Algeria in Turmoil*,
an entire army corps could have been wasted.

> It was apparent from the start that a modern striking force
> was ill-suited to conditions in the Aurès. Heavily equipped units
> dependent on motor transport lost much of their mobility in the
> hills and were easily out-maneuvered. . . . The rebels, slithering
> through the thousand gullies and defiles of a region the size of
> Connecticut and as wild as the Mountains of the Moon, had every
> advantage; they could have eluded an army corps.

And did. The tactics practiced by Mao in China, by Giap in
Indochina, were pursued in the seven-year struggle to follow,
and little is learned by detailing them.

As in Indochina, the Algerian rebels of the National Liberation Front (F.L.N.) and its allies proved that if they could not
decisively defeat a modern army, neither could they be defeated.
Although fortunes varied from year to year, and those of the
F.L.N. were at low ebb when General de Gaulle finally threw in
the sponge in 1962, resistance never ceased at any time, extending from the Aurès to deep in the Sahara over 847,000 square
miles of battleground that all the armies of the world could not
have "pacified"—to use the French expression.

The ruthless use of torture and counter-terror—a scandal in
France—proved that *urban* rebellions *can* be crushed. The city of
Algiers was brought under control by massive policing, with the
aid of the large French population of *colons*. But the Aurès and
other mountainous regions served as guerrilla sanctuaries until
the end: A year after the French withdrawal, dissident Berber
forces in the mountains were seen offering defiance to the revolutionary government established by the F.L.N.!

A clear-cut military decision was impossible. The accomplish-
ment of the Algerian guerrillas, successfully defying French

forces a million strong, was to create a drain on French man-power and the French treasury that was too great, given the do-mestic political dissension on the Algerian question that existed, for even a major industrial and military power to bear.

The protracted war in Algeria finally brought Paris to a pain-ful choice: French prestige, the natural wealth of Algeria, and the political weight of a million *colons* on the one hand; political turmoil, continued frustration, and a deadly drain on the na-tional economy on the other.

The war of the flea had bled France to the point of grave eco-nomic anemia and produced a raging political fever that was bringing the home country itself to the brink of revolution. De-Gaulle, brought to power in the hope that he would somehow solve the Algerian crisis, opted for peace in North Africa at the risk of war with the very military leaders who had chosen him. The French people, drained and sickened by seven years of senseless slaughter in a land still foreign after a century and a quarter of colonization, supported him in his gamble. There was a bloody denouement to come, as the military and the *colons* rebelled, but it proved nothing, changed nothing. The French *presence* was withdrawn, and a new flag flew over an indepen-dent Algeria.

A footnote: From Algiers the war of the flea spreads south-ward. Algerian weapons arm Congolese rebels against an army led by white mercenaries, and Premier ben Bella, defying the Western bloc, declares that his regime will aid wars of national liberation wherever they may arise.

# GENERAL GRIVAS ON GUERRILLA WAR IN CYPRUS. THE POLITICAL USES OF TERRORISM. ERRORS OF BRITISH STRATEGY.

"The British, who arm their commandoes with knives and instruct them to kill . . . from the rear—protested vigorously when such tactics were applied to themselves. It may be argued that these things are only permissible in war. This is nonsense. I was fighting a war in Cyprus against the British, and if they did not recognize the fact from the start they were forced to at the end. The truth is that our form of war, in which a few hundred fell in four years, was more selective than most, and I speak as one who has seen battlefields covered with dead. We did not strike, like the bomber, at random. We shot only British servicemen who would have killed us if they could have fired first, and civilians who were traitors or intelligence agents. To shoot down your enemies in the street may be unprecedented, but I was looking for results, not precedents. How did Napoleon win his victories? He took his opponents in the flank or rear; and what is right on the grand scale is not wrong when the scale is reduced and the odds against you are a hundred to one."*

The words are from *Memoirs* of the EOKA† leader, General George Grivas; the subject, terror.

Although Grivas is the archetype of the conservative military

* *The Memoirs of General Grivas;* Frederick A. Praeger, Inc.
†EOKA: Ethniki Organosis Kyprion Agoniston [National Organization of Cypriot Fighters]. General Grivas is now commander-in-chief of the Republic of Cyprus' National Guard.

man—a jingo and a fascist in the eyes of the Greek Communists—his philosophy of terrorism approaches that of the anarchists. The state exercises authority by the use of threat of force,
argue the anarchists: The policeman on the corner is the agent
as well as the symbol of it, and the revolver at his side is there to
intimidate or, in the extremity, to kill those who resist him. If
then his authority is illicit, being exercised without the just consent of the governed, is it no right and natural to oppose force
with force, to kill policemen as one would kill bandits, and to
combat usurpers as one would combat an invasion?

In effect, this was the reasoning that led Grivas, a Greek Cypriot, to declare war on the British rulers of Greek (and Turkish)
Cyprus.

In his *Memoirs* he writes that it was "with deep regret, but
with a high sense of duty" that he took up arms in 1955 against
an old friend and ally, Britain. He blames, not the British people,
but "a band of politicians" who denied even the hope of freedom to Cyprus, and he adds: "It is on their heads that the guilt
rests for the death of so many men, women and children in the
tragic years that followed."

The beginning of the Cypriot struggle for independence was
announced, March 31, 1955, by a series of explosions across the
island. Saboteurs raiding the government radio station in Nicosia set off bombs that wrecked the broadcasting equipment
and lifted the roof from the building, causing damage estimated
at £60,000. Bombs were thrown into government office buildings
and into wireless installations at the Wolseley Barracks, headquarters of a British military force which at that time numbered
only four thousand men. In the port of Limassol, a power plant
and the two main police stations were bombed. At Larnaca, the
police headquarters, the courts, and the British Commissioner's
office all were shattered by bomb blasts.

The first casualty of the campaign occurred in Famagusta—a
member of an EOKA group was electrocuted when he threw a
damp rope over a high-tension power line in an attempt to sabotage the electrical supply.

The attack took the world by surprise; colonial officials were
stunned and panic-stricken, says Grivas.

The wave of bombing attacks was coupled with more general political action. Young students and school children were rapidly recruited into the independent movement—"I intended to turn the youth of Cyprus into the seedbed of EOKA," writes Grivas—and a series of successful demonstrations was organized, sufficiently violent to drive police from the streets and to require the use of soldiers to restore order.

Children as young as ten years old were used to distribute EOKA leaflets and to act as couriers; teachers who interfered in disregard of the Organization's warning were punished "severely," a phrase that, as Grivas employed it, usually meant shooting by EOKA execution squads.

Pressure was put on Cypriot newspapers that were slow to take the right tone with regard to the campaign; for example, newspapers that failed to denounce the passage of repressive laws. Those of "weak spirit" soon felt the weight of the EOKA boycott.

The wave of terrorism had been initiated by an extremely small group of men—not more than eighty, according to Grivas, organized into sabotage squads of five or six in all of the principal cities and towns of the island. There were, as yet, no guerrilla units, although Grivas has personally reconnoitered the island, making notes of favorable places for ambushes, terrain suitable to provide bases for guerrilla action, and so on.

The excellent network of roads across the island militated against an extensive guerrilla campaign, and most of those who were to fight as guerrillas were not sent into the countryside until they had outlived their usefulness in the towns, by becoming too well known to risk being seen in the streets. The mountains of the Kyrenia range and the heavily wooded Troodos range in the southwest were, however, subsequently used as bases of guerrilla operations and for the training of sabotage teams.

After the first outbreak of bombings, there was a lull in the terror campaign, broken for some weeks only by isolated attacks against what Grivas calls "targets of opportunity." One of these, according to the *Memoirs,* was Sir Robert Armitage, the British governor of Cyprus.

As part of Empire Day celebrations in Nicosia, the governor attended a film premiere at the Pallas Cinema. He sat throughout the showing, for two hours, only a few feet from a seat under which a time-pencil attached to a Coca-Cola bottle filled with explosive slowly burned. The picture ended. The governor and his party left the theater. Five minutes later, the bomb exploded, shattering seven rows of vacant seats and riddling the ceiling with shrapnel.

Grivas spent the time between attacks traveling about Nicosia, and on occasion into the Kyrenia mountains, giving orders to group leaders, supervising training, preparing propaganda releases, and generally bolstering morale by his appearances. His identity as "Dighenis, the Leader"—the way in which he invariably signed his communiques—had already been revealed. The small Cypriot Community Party had denounced EOKA as "hooligans" and "pop-gun wielders." (The Party line recalls that taken in Cuba, where the Communists denounced Fidel Castro and his suppoerters as "bourgeois putschists.") Taking the same cue, the leader of the Greek Communist Party disclosed in a broadcast from Moscow that Dighenis was Grivas, well known to the Communists as the leader of the Greek underground organization of World War II called "Xhi," and later as a commander of Greek army operations against the Communist guerrillas of ELAS in the Greek civil war.

"Comically, the British did not take this piece of information seriously," recalls Grivas. "The idea of an elderly retired officer as the Leader of EOKA was too strange for them to accept." "Dighenis" continued to move about freely, in the thin disguise of dark glasses and a clipped moustache. For a time he established a headquarters in the mountains, but later, he relates, he hid in a house in Limassol for two years without being discovered or betrayed.

EOKA's second wave of attacks came in June. The first victim of the campaign wa a policeman killed when a bomb blew a hole in the wall of the divisional police headquarters in Nicosia. Sixteen men were wounded. A sergeant was killed when an assault group attacked the Amiandos police station, and several other stations were attacked. Grivas had personally selected a target: the Commander in Chief of British land forces in the Middle East, General Keightley, who was accustomed to drive daily into the capital from his home on the Kyrenia coast. "I found a good place for an ambush on the pass over the Kyrenia mountains," writes Grivas, "but Archbishop Makarios vetoed the plan and the idea was abandoned."

The *Memoirs* reveal that Makarios vetoed a good many plans proposed by the Leader, and often dragged his feet when Grivas would have forged boldly ahead. The Archbishop held the pursestrings; without funds Grivas was unable to proceed and was forced to reconsider some of his more drastic schemes, as, for example, when he wished to send execution squads to London to assassinate known Cypriot informers living in Britain on the rewards of their betrayals.

In general, however, the campaign proceeded as Grivas wished it to, with the Leader maintaining a rigid discipline over his scattered troops of terrorists and saboteurs. "I issued frequent warnings that I alone would give orders: disobedience would be punished by death."

Although Grivas says that at the onset he would have been able, given five hundred armed men, to drive the British into the sea, the remark is not to be taken seriously. From the start, he saw very clearly that his victory would be political rather than military. This is made clear in the general plan which he drew up in Athens two years before the first bomb exploded in Nicosia.

I. THE OBJECTIVE

To arouse international public opinion, especially among the allies of Greece, by deeds of heroism and self-sacrifice which will focus attention on Cyprus until our aims are achieved. The British must be continuously harried and beset until they are obliged by international diplomacy exercised through the United Nations to examine the Cyprus problem and settle it in accordance with the desires of the Cypriot people and the whole Greek nation.

II. THE PROCEDURE

Activity will be aimed at causing so much confusion and damage in the ranks of the British forces as to make it manifest abroad that they are no longer in complete control of the situation. The campaign will be carried out on three fronts:

1. Sabotage against Government installations and military posts.
2. Attacks on British forces by a considerable number of armed fighting groups.
3. Organization of passive resistance by the population.

Because of the difficulties in the way of a large-scale guerrilla struggle . . . the main weight of the campaign will be placed on sabotage, and therefore the chief task of the fighting groups will be to support and cover the work of saboteurs by upsetting and diverting the Government forces. . . . Success will not be achieved by minor and intermittent attacks but only by a continuous campaign aimed at getting important results. It should not be supposed that by these means we should expect to impose a total material defeat on the British forces; our purpose is to bring about a moral defeat by keeping up the offensive until the objectives stated in the first paragraph of this plan are realised.

By the end of June, 1955, the second phase of the campaign had ended. EOKA fighters were informed in a bulletin that the "material results" had not been up to the expectations of the Leader. There had been few casualties and the damage caused by the sabotage had been relatively insignificant from the economic point of view. Presumably it was this to which Grivas referred when he spoke of "material results."

In political terms, however, the EOKA campaign had already achieved a considerable measure of success. The primary purpose of the organization was being realized. The issue of self-determination for Cyprus had been called dramatically to the attention of the world. British public opinion, in particular, had been aroused, and with the anticipated results: The policy of a government that had said it could NEVER consider Cypriot independence—Cyprus supposedly being indispensable to Britain's military security in the Mediterranean—was being questioned; and there were already second thoughts about the word "never."

Two years earlier, the British had refused to discuss Cyprus with the Greek government. Now, the Prime Minister, Sir Anthony Eden, sent invitations to both Athens and Ankara to attend a tripartite conference in London. Archbishop Makarios, seeking a larger forum and a better solution than could be expected from any such meeting, flew to Athens to press the Greek government to appeal to the United Nations. Before leaving he sent Grivas his congratulations, adding:

"EOKA has contributed infinitely more to the Cyprus struggle than 75 years of paper war. The name of Dighenis is an enigma to the British. And it is a legend as well. Already it has passed into the pages of the liberation movement's history."

Grivas was preparing a general attack timed to coincide with the meeting of the United Nations General Assembly in the fall. As an initial step, he proposed to put the native police force out of action as a reliable law enforcement agency, so as to compel the British to extend their military forces, which were being used mainly to guard government buildings or held in their barracks for riot duty and similar emergencies.

In an order dated June 28, he informed EOKA group leaders:

The aim of our next offensive will be to terrorize the police and to paralyze the administration, both in the towns and the countryside. If this aim is achieved, the results will be threefold:

Disillusionment will spread through the Police Force so rapidly that most of them, if they do not actually help us, will turn a blind eye to our activities.

Active intervention of the Army in security, which will stretch the troops and tire them out. The falling morale of the Army will also influence its leaders.

In the face of our strength and persistence and the trouble they cause, it is very probable that the United Nations, through member countries who take an interest in Cyprus affairs, will seek to bring about a solution.

The results we want will be obtained by:

1. Murderous attacks against policemen who are out of sympathy with our aims or who try to hunt us down.

2. Ambushes against police patrols in towns or raids on country police stations.

3. Obstructing free movement of the police across the island by laying ambushes (against individuals or groups).

The police were given notice of what to expect in a leaflet posted on walls in the villages and scattered through the city streets by schoolchildren:

TO THE POLICE: I have warned you and I shall carry out my warning to the letter. Darker days await the tyrants of Cyprus, heavier punishments the traitors. . . . Do not try to block our path or you will stain it with your blood. I have given orders that:

> Anyone who tries to stop the Cypriot patriots will be EXECUTED.
> Anyone who tries to arrest or to search Cypriot patriots will be SHOT.

YOU HAVE NOTHING TO FEAR SO LONG AS YOU DO NOT GET IN OUR WAY.

EOKA,
The Leader,
Dighenis.

Having given warning, EOKA proceeded with a series of raids on police stations that served a twofold purpose: The attacks frightened the police and also gave the organization a means of getting badly needed arms, since few were arriving from Greece, where the first weapons and supplies had been obtained.

The campaign in the towns lagged, a fact Grivas explains almost apologetically, was "due to the total inexperience of the execution groups." Results were nevertheless obtained. Several policemen were killed and others wounded in Nicosia and Famagusta. Scores resigned; and those who remained, says Grivas, scarcely dared show their faces outside of their stations. The effect of the raids was to throw the administration entirely on the defensive. Armed sentries walked around and around the police stations at night, and when the police had to close a station temporarily, they took all of their weapons with them.

The British knew next to nothing about EOKA—who its members were, where they might be found. Those who might have been able to tell them, the Greek Cypriot members of the police force, were soon silenced.

On August 28, a constable of the Special Branch who had been marked for death because of his "too zealous" application to duty was posted at a political meeting in Ledra Street in Nicosia. He was shot down before a crowd of hundreds by a young government clerk, Michael Karaolis, a member of a three-man EOKA execution squad.

The killing in broad daylight before hundreds of people in the heart of the capital was a fatal blow to police morale. The killer, Karaolis, was later caught and sentenced to death, but his work had been done. The slaying of the Special Branch man, says Grivas, "shattered opposition to EOKA among the Greek police."

Increasingly, Turks were recruited to replace Greeks on the police force, intensifying the hostility between the two ethnic communities. Of the Greeks who remained on the British payroll, many became spies for EOKA, accurately informing the organization of British intentions from day to day. Those who were not so employed closed their eyes to EOKA activities, as Grivas had predicted, and ceased to be of effective service to the British, or a hindrance to the liberation movement.

British propaganda was bitter in its denunciation of the methods used by EOKA, but Grivas was not concerned. As he later wrote:

> All war is cruel and the only way to win against superior force is by ruse and trickery; you can no more afford to make a difference between striking in front or striking from behind than you can between employing rifles and howitzers. The British may criticise me as much as they like for making war in Cyprus, but I was not obliged to ask their permission to do so; nor can they now deny that I made it in the most successful way.

\* \* \*

Terrorism was supported by intensive political agitation that brought out huge crowds in the principal towns. During one demonstration in Nicosia in September, army trucks were overturned and set afire and the British Institute was burned to the ground.

The headlines generated by this activity failed to win Greece a hearing on the Cyprus question in the United Nations. The

Greek appeal was rejected on September 23. But the EOKA campaign had shaken the British. Two days after the U.N. rejection, it was announced in London that a new governor would replace Sir Robert Armitage immediately.

The replacement was the much-decorated Field Marshal Sir John Harding, an outstanding British general of World War II who had just relinquished the post of chief of the Imperial General Staff. "He was, in fact," writes Grivas, "the leading British soldier of his day, and no higher compliment could have been paid us than to send against our tiny forces a man with so great a reputation and so brilliant a career."

Harding, as it developed, was to have no better success against EOKA than had his predecessor.

The appointment of a military man to replace the civilian governor made it clear that Downing Street intended to stamp out EOKA by main force, rather than to continue a police acation. The trouble, as is usually the case when opposing guerrillas, and even more so when fighting terrorists, was that there was nothing substantial against which to apply the force. As Grivas explains:

> The British answer to our methods was to flood the island with troops. It was the wrong answer. Numbers have little meaning in guerrilla warfare. From the guerrillas' point of view, it is positively dangerous to increase the size of groups beyond a certain point. I call this the "saturation point." It is determined by the nature of the terrain, the skill of the fighters, their requirements in food and supplies, the tactics employed and the need to keep down casualties. Any given area can usefully absorb a certain number of men; in mountainous country, where peaks and ravines are dead ground, the figure is only a fraction of the numbers required elsewhere. I myself, when I joined the *andartes* in the mountains always felt uneasy if there were more than half a dozen of us together. Even in the plains the saturation point is lower than one might suppose: for example, to use more than five or six men in a village attack would serve no purpose, for the more numerous the attackers, the more difficult it is for them to escape after the action. On the same principle, villages where we were strong pretended inertia, on my orders, until it was appropriate

for them to strike, while others, where our forces were weaker, continued to attack repeatedly, simply to deceive the enemy. If this led to arrests, even of a whole group, it was not important, for there was always a complete reserve group waiting to fill their places. Thus I never disclosed my full strength to the enemy, but after each sudden eruption of violence left an empty battlefield. When the British tried to strike back, they found nothing to strike at. This was the secret of my success throughout four years of hard fighting, and my principles did not change when Harding came on the scene.*

It is well to remember that Grivas is talking about a campaign based primarily on terrorism and sabotage, fought on a small island affording little space for maneuver, and aimed at political rather than military effect. He was not trying to build self-sustaining guerrilla base areas, or to reach the ultimate guerrilla goal (impossible in Cyprus) of an equalization of military forces. In terms of Cyprus, small guerrilla units could be treated as expendable; they were expendable in precisely the way that terrorists are expendable, who do not seek to build a military force, but rather to produce political and psychological effects, often by sacrificing themselves.

Grivas cleverly used his urban and rural groups in interaction: When he wished to conduct a campaign in the countryside, he raised big political demonstrations in the towns that kept the troops occupied there on riot duty, while his guerrilla groups made lightning attacks on rural objectives. When he was planning a new drive in the cities, he created diversions in the countryside that brought the troops out in intensive *ratissages.*

"... my resources were meagre and I could not hope to win a military victory;" he writes, "it was rather a question of raising a force and keeping it in being no matter what the enemy did to destroy it. This, and more, was achieved in the first six months."

On his arrival in Nicosia, Harding made a cursory attempt to negotiate with Archbishop Makarios. When the negotiations broke down within a few days, Grivas ordered a full-scale EOKA offensive. New attacks were launched against village po-

*The Memoirs of General Grivas.*

lice stations in an effort to draw out the army. EOKA men raided the Mitsero mine and escaped with fifteen hundred sticks of dynamite, six hundred detonators, and three thousand yards of fuse. Another raiding party invaded the military warehouses in Famagusta harbor, bound and gagged a watchman, and drove off with a truckload of British arms—Bren guns, Stens, mortars, and bazookas.

Political agitation was intensified, and the British worsened the situation for themselves by ill-advised attempts to prevent public demonstrations. The timing of the announcement that Michael Karaolis, "the first hero of the revolution," had been sentenced to death, could not have been worse. The announcement came on October 28, a national holiday marking the refusal of Greece to surrender to the Axis powers in 1940. Harding banned any sort of public demonstration; Grivas responded by calling on Cypriots to defy the ban, and a series of bloody clashes resulted. Troops opened fire on a riotous crowd, wounding three men, and there were more than a thousand arrests, jamming the jails of the principal towns, as the result of street fighting.

With British forces occupied in the towns by demonstrations and sabotage, Grivas ordered an island-wide assault. It began on November 18, when more than fifty bombs were thrown in thirty separate attacks throughout Cyprus. By the end of a week, several hundred attacks had been carried out. The main post office in Nicosia was bombed—the bomb simply dropped in the letter box—and half the building was destroyed. An eight-pound bomb carried into the Kykko military encampment outside of Nicosia in the saddlebag of a bicycle blew the roof off the warrant officers' and sergeants' mess and killed two sergeants. Army posts at Limassol and Larnaca were attacked. Guerrillas in the Kyrenia Range attacked two mines and engaged in fire fights with the troops detailed to guard them. Mine company trucks carrying dynamite were ambushed, and near Famagusta three military vehicles were blasted off the road, causing the army to stop all military movements on the roads at night.

Grivas himself led an ambush attack on two army trucks, destroyed one, and then withdrew with his squad to a nearby hilltop and calmly watched as a relief party, which did not appear until three hours after the attack, removed the body of a dead soldier from the wreckage. No attempt was made to search the area.

A state of emergency was declared throughout the island on November 26. Police were given extraordinary powers of search and arrest. Strikes were forbidden. The death penalty was imposed for carrying arms, and saboteurs were liable to life imprisonment. British troops, responding to the assassination of their comrades in arms much as the Black and Tans had done in Ireland, vented their feelings on the civilian population. Soldiers stopped farm trucks on the way to market and dumped their loads of fruit and vegetables out on the road. Search parties invaded private homes, abused the occupants, and destroyed their possessions. Suspects were arrested without warrant and held for weeks or months in detention camps without trial. "The 'security forces' set about their work," comments Grivas, "in a manner which might have been deliberately designed to drive the population into our arms." It had that effect.

\* \* \*

Grivas had gone into the Troodos mountains to coordinate guerrilla operations, and on several occasions he narrowly escaped British commandos combing the area where he happened to be hiding. On one occasion, two British forces totaling seven hundred men, lost in the mist on a mountainside, closed in on each other as the guerrillas escaped, and engaged in a battle with each other that lasted for an hour before they discovered that they were firing on their own troops. There were more than fifty casualties.

On New Year's Day of 1956, Harding broadcast the prediction that "the days of EOKA are numbered." The following day, eight hundred British troops closed in on a woods where Grivas was thought to be, spent the entire day combing an area two miles square, and withdrew with three prisoners. Grivas reports: "I was, in fact, a few miles south of the operations area, watching the progress of the search through binoculars. I was astonished at the unmethodical way the troops went about their work."

On the 22nd of the month, EOKA units simultaneously raided every village on Cyprus, in an effort to gather up all of the several thousand shotguns on the island that were registered with the police. One EOKA man was wounded and a soldier was killed in the raids; more than eight hundred shotguns were seized, and Grivas proceeded to organize special shotgun units: "These were used to harry the British by night, attack army camps, create diversions for major guerrilla attacks, and execute traitors."

By February of 1956, the strength of the army had been increased from four thousand to some twenty-two thousand men. EOKA by this time had a total "front-line strength" of two hundred seventy-three men, supported by some seven hundred fifty part-time guerrillas in the villages, armed only with shotguns. The "front-line" fighters included eighty men divided into fifteen groups in Nicosia, seventy-six men in Famagusta, and thirty-four men in Limassol, the three principal towns of the island. The numerical odds were vastly in favor of the British, but Grivas considered the army, supported by five thousand police, "a cumbersome body" that "provided a wealth of targets, new and old, in both town and mountain." So it proved.

Grivas intensified his campaign of terror and sabotage. The homes of British senior officers were bombed, British servicemen were shot down in the streets, bombs were tossed into clubs and taverns frequented by troops. A servant who belonged to EOKA even succeeded in planting a bomb under the mattress of Sir John Harding's bed: fortunately for the governor, a sudden change in the temperature (so Grivas explains) affected the time pencil, and the bomb did not explode until after it had been discovered and removed.

The British seemed to have learned little or nothing from their previous experience of terrorism elsewhere. Efforts to intimidate the civilian population that aided EOKA only embittered it. The experiment of imposing collective fines on the Greek community in reprisal against attacks on British forces—the levies ranged from a few hundred pounds in some small villages to £40,000 in

Famagusta and £35,000 in Limassol—was abandoned after six months as ineffective.

Stern measures against captured EOKA fighters not only failed to act as a deterrent, but created severe political repercussions. When the first of the EOKA gunmen to be executed were hanged for murder in Central Prison, Nicosia, on May 10, 1956, huge demonstrations in Greece were called in protest, seven persons were killed in a riot in Athens, and the mayor of that city solemnly hammered to pieces a marble plaque dedicated to Queen Elizabeth and Prince Philip before the eyes of a cheering crowd. Even the British press condemned the hangings. No doubt sympathy was felt for the two British hostages whom Grivas had executed by EOKA the next day in reprisal for the executions, but the headlines had already been spent on what millions evidently considered a miscarriage of British justice. It is an irony of political warfare—and a political fact to be considered and understood—that the rules are not the same for both sides.

British troops fared no better against the EOKA guerrillas in the countryside than against the terrorists in the towns. The troops burned thousands of acres of timber in scattered efforts to flush out guerrilla bands on the mountainsides, but few guerrillas were caught, and those were quickly replaced by others.

> Harding tried to strike back at the mountain groups [writes Grivas], but, lacking any comprehensive plan and failing to grasp our methods, he had few successes. His activities were dependent on spasmodic tips from informers, which were often inexact and unreliable and led him to concentrate on narrow zones: as many as fifty truckloads of troops would be poured into one small area, which would be searched for a day; but nearly always we slipped away before the search began and watched its progress from the neighboring heights, certain that they would not extend the operation beyond its original limits.

What *should* have been done? Examining his opponent's problem in retrospect, Grivas says:

> . . . Harding persisted in his error: he underrated his enemy on the one hand, and overweighted his forces on the other. But one

does not use a tank to catch field-mice—a cat will do the job better. The Field-Marshal's only hope of finding us was to play cat and mouse: to use tiny, expertly trained groups, who could work with cunning and patience and strike rapidly when we least expected.

No such groups were ever developed, and the war continued along the lines and with the results that might have been expected. What Harding was unable to accomplish with twenty thousand troops in 1956 could not be accomplished by his successor with twice that many in 1958. Forty-three thousand British soldiers were on Cyprus when the shooting ended, but what they were doing there, few could have said. Certainly they were not keeping the peace.

Grivas offers his record of EOKA activities for October 2, 1958, as giving an idea of the scale of operations at that time:

LARNACA: Soldier killed by bomb; civilian agent dead by execution squad.
NICOSIA: Bomb thrown into police headquarters from car, casualties unknown.
FAMAGUSTA: Two army trucks ambushed, casualties unknown.
LIMASSOL: Eight Britons injured by bomb at Acropole Hotel; four soldiers injured by bomb thrown at truck.
PLATANI: Two soldiers killed, two wounded in mined truck.
PANAYIA-STAVROS: Two soldiers killed, two wounded in ambush.
PYROI: Truck ambushed, casualties unknown.
MESOYI: Two soldiers killed in ambush of truck.
PIYI: Two soldiers killed, two wounded in mined truck.
PERISTERONA: Bombs thrown at two army trucks, casualties unknown.

The British authorities embittered the struggle but did little to change its course by involving the Turkish community in the fighting. The recruitment of Turks into the police and the incitement of latent racial antagonisms produced some bloody civilian massacres and a tragic toll of innocent lives on both sides; but divide-and-rule as an instrument of British policy failed in Cyprus.

The eventual political settlement that was reached in the Zurich and London agreements, establishing the Republic of Cyprus under a constitution written by London, Athens, and Ankara, was less than satisfactory to Grivas. He had fought for the independence of the island as a step toward union with Greece, *enosis,* and this was denied.

But the British could scarcely claim to have won even a partial victory. They had paid a heavy price in money, lives, and prestige during four years of futile fighting, and had nothing to show for it but a paper compromise that was worse than outright defeat: Where there had been a troublesome colonial question, an explosive international issue was created, and one that remains to date a grave threat to peace in the Mediterranean, a threat not least of all to the British themselves.

As to the conflict that led to Zurich, it was, round by round, a series of clear defeats for colonial arms and colonial policies. The British proceeded against EOKA as against a band of ordinary criminals, relying on the methods that would be used to put down an outbreak of banditry and seeming never to realize what had been perfectly clear to Grivas from the start:

"I laughed aloud when I read that General A or Brigadier B had come to Cyprus to put into operation the methods that had won him fame elsewhere. They could not understand that the Cyprus struggle was unique in motive, psychology and circumstance, *and involved not a handful of insurrectionists but the whole people.*"

## FAILURES IN THE WAR OF THE FLEA. MAGSAYSAY AND THE HUKS IN THE PHILIPPINES. THE PRICE OF BRITISH VICTORY IN MALAYA. WHY THE COMMUNISTS LOST IN GREECE.

Mao's analogy of the guerrilla, swimming like a fish in the sea of the population, is so often repeated because it contains an essential truth: It expresses accurately as well as picturesquely the fundamental principle of guerrilla war. Carry the analogy a step farther, and ask what happens when the fish is removed—or removes himself—from the water. The answer explains, better than a treatise, the reason for the failure of the few guerrilla movements that have been successfully suppressed.

The destruction in 1949 of the Greek Communist guerrilla forces of the Democratic Army is a prime example. Malaya is another. The Hukbalahap insurrection in the Philippines is, perhaps, a third. All three show what happens when guerrillas are cut off, or deliberately cut themselves off (as the Greek Communists did) from popular contact and support.

The Huk movement, which like so many others had its origin in World War II, offers more instruction to the counterinsurgency strategists than do the others, because it exemplifies the successful use of political and social rather than military weapons against guerrillas.

Credits for the success of the Philippine pacification campaign seems to go largely to a single intelligent politician, the late President Ramon Magsaysay, who became Secretary of National Defense in 1950, at a time when the Huks appeared almost on the point of invading Manila itself.

The Huks, like the Vietminh in Indochina, ELAS in Greece, the Malayan Communists, and other insurgents in Axis-held territory throughout the world during World War II, had come into being as a patriotic force—nationalist guerrillas opposing a foreign invader—with the blessings, practical instruction, and material aid of the Allied powers, specifically of the United States. But revolutionary motivations are complex: The Huks had been fighting *for* something as well as *against* something. Wartime slogans had been taken seriously and, with the war over and the Japanese driven from the islands, social aspirations eclipsed even independence, granted conditionally in 1946, as a motivating force. The men who had been fighting the Japanese were now fighting for themselves: They demanded a political voice and a share of the land for which they had fought.

Magsaysay, a former guerrilla himself, was clever enough to see what was required, and influential enough to get it.

When he took office in 1950, the Huks, dominating central Luzon and much of Mindanao, the second largest island of the chain, commanded some 12,000 armed guerrillas and had the active cooperation of an estimated one million Filipinos in a nation of seventeen million. An army of thirty thousand soldiers was helpless to contain them; the stockpiles of weapons captured from the Japanese or supplied during the war by the United States would have been sufficient to keep a civil war in progress for decades, and the bulk of the population, if not actively sympathetic to the insurgents, was, at least, passive.

The terrain—mountains and swampy jungle—favored the guerrillas. The troops, hated by the villagers, were confined to the larger centers of population and were seldom seen in the back country except on sporadic punitive expeditions, and then only in full force, an invading army arriving in trucks and armored vehicles to terrorize the rural population.

Magsaysay's first step was to reorganize the army and put an end to military terrorism. Pressure against the Huks was increased by sending out small armed units, functioning more like constabulary than troops, to hunt down the guerrillas piecemeal, while devoting most of the army to social work—setting up medical stations, building schoolhouses, repairing roads and bridges, helping the peasants get their rice to market.

His second step—and the first would have been useless without it—was to obtain legislation that made it possible to offer the Huks what they had been fighting for, on the condition that they lay down their arms. An amnesty was proclaimed and the Communist slogan, "Land for the Landless," was subverted by an agrarian reform and resettlement program under which any guerrilla who surrendered was given a plot of his own.

Clever bribery worked where other inducements did not. Substantial bounties were paid for weapons. Rewards were put on the heads of key Huk leaders, and subsequent betrayals disrupted the direction of the guerrilla campaign, cutting the roving bands off from their urban base in Manila, where virtually the entire rebel political directorate was captured.

In 1951, troops were set to guard the ballot boxes as an honest election (possibly the first in Filipino history) was conducted, leading to further social reforms that progressively weakened the Communist appeal.

By the time the Huk leader, Luis Taroc, surrendered in 1954, the rural villages were firmly in the hands of the government, and the Huks had been reduced, more by defections than otherwise, to a few thousands, scattered over the less accessible mountain and jungle areas of the two main islands.

They still had not been defeated militarily—indeed, they have not been entirely eliminated to this day and lately they have shown signs of reviving—but they had lost the propaganda war and their popular appeal; their cause had been stolen from them by a government far more popular (thanks in part to an economy bolstered by $620,000,000 of American aid) than any that had ruled before; and thus they had been isolated slowly but surely from the support on which their successful existence depended.

It is a matter of speculation whether the Huks could not have accomplished more by better exploiting their strength when they had it. One of their signal weaknesses seems to have been their failure to establish anything like a popular front during a period when urban support, the participation of students, industrial workers, and the poorer white-collar class, was clearly required. The insurrection was a peasant movement, and remained confined to the rural areas. Although the guerrillas dominated the villages in 1949–50, they never seriously disrupted the economy of the islands or the life of the capital. Their tactics in the field, mainly evasive, failed to produce the kind of results that could be exploited in terms of propaganda for major political effect; and once deprived of political leadership they seem to have lapsed into an existence hardly to be distinguished from banditry, surrendering the political as well as the military initiative to Manila.

Militarily, a force of twelve thousand guerrillas with strong support in the countryside, opposed by a relatively small army of only thirty thousand men, should have been able to concentrate sufficient strength in any given place to reduce any but the strongest of garrisons or to capture any but the largest of towns. The Huks failed to do so.

As saboteurs, they should have been able to initiate an aggressive campaign of destruction that would have crippled communications and paralyzed the national economy. Far smaller forces have done it elsewhere—but again the Huks failed.

Unwilling or psychologically unable to take the initiative, they failed to seize and hold the popular imagination and so to create the broad mass unrest needed to topple the government or to build a revolutionary army capable of confronting and defeating the government army. "Public opinion," says Clausewitz, "is ultimately gained by great victories." The Huks needed, if not great victories, then a strong foretaste of success in order to create the bandwagon effect on which successful revolutionary movements are built.

They had made a good start, but they failed to exploit it. Magsaysay's reforms came in time to blunt the edge of popular grievances and to broaden the political base of the regime while narrowing that of the Huk movement to the point where it was virtually eliminated as a revolutionary force.

\* \* \*

In postwar Malaya, the situation was radically different from that of the Philippines, despite certain obvious similarities. There was a strong Communist guerrilla movement. As in the Philippines, it had been schooled by experts; indeed, Chin Peng, the secretary-general of the Malayan Communist Party, had been described during the war as "Britain's most trusted guerrilla," and some two hundred Party members had learned irregular warfare, a few years earlier, in the British army's special training school in Singapore.

In addition, there was an extensive political organization, the Min Yuen, or Masses' Movement, reaching into virtually every town and village of any consequence on the Malayan Peninsula.

Unfortunately for the Communists, however, the so-called Malayan Races Liberation Army (MRLA), had very few Malayans in it, being composed almost exclusively of Chinese, and more particularly, of the large squatter population of recent Chinese immigrants, with no deep roots in the country.

The guerrillas, with a total strength variously estimated at five thousand to ten thousand, were able to launch a campaign of terrorism and sabotage that was initially effective. But their weakness in the long run lay in the comparative ease with which they could be isolated.

The jungle in which they necessarily found refuge was inhabited not by farmers, but by tribal aborigines scarcely able to grow enough food to support themselves. Consequently, the food on which the guerrillas relied had to be smuggled from the villages, through the Min Yuen network, and this was soon halted by vigilant police activity.

A massive and costly resettlement program removed more than half a million Chinese squatters, mostly tin mine and rubber plantation workers, from their shacks on the fringe of the jungle to protected villages, where they could be kept under surveillance and at the same time offered advantages that tended to woo them from their political connection with the insurgents.

The latter, cut off from contact with the mass of the population, lacking the material support of even the Chinese community on which they had relied, were then slowly starved into submission or lured into ambushes in which they were reduced piecemeal.

The resettlement program, the prototype of the protected-villages experiment in South Viet Nam, is of some interest to counterinsurgency specialists, as are some of the methods developed by the British to combat the Chinese guerrillas in the Malayan jungle.

What is of principal interest in the Malayan experience, however, is not the defeat of the MRLA—a foredoomed effort, in any event—but the duration of the suppression campaign and its extremely high cost.

Despite the obvious handicaps under which they fought, the Chinese Communist guerrillas in Malaya still had not been eliminated as a fighting force a full ten years after the struggle began; indeed, a few hundred guerrillas still survive in the jungle, although they are no longer considered dangerous.

During the ten years they fought, they tied up British forces one hundred forty thousand strong, including forty thousand regular troops and about one hundred thousand regular and auxiliary police.

The expense of the military effort can be judged by the following detailed account of "Operation Nassau," described as typical of battalion-sized British counterguerrilla operations in Malaya:

Operation Nassau . . . began in December, 1954, and ended in September, 1955. The South Swamp of Kuala Langat covers an area of over 100 square miles. It is a dense jungle with trees up to 150 feet tall where visibility is limited to about thirty yards. After several assassinations, a British battalion was assigned to the area. Food control was achieved through a system of rationing, convoys, gate checks, and searches. One company began operations in the swamp about December 21, 1954. On January 9, 1955, full-scale tactical operations began; artillery, mortars, and aircraft began harassing fires in South Swamp. Originally, the plan was to bomb and shell the swamp day and night so that the terrorists would be driven out into ambushes; but the terrorists were well prepared to stay indefinitely. Food parties came out occasionally, but the civil population was too afraid to report them.

Plans were modified; harassing fires were reduced to night-time only. Ambushes continued and patrolling inside the swamp was intensified. Operations of this nature continued for three months without results. Finally on March 21, an ambush party, after forty-five hours of waiting, succeeded in killing two of eight terrorists. The first two red pins, signifying kills, appeared on the operations map, and local morale rose a little.

Another month passed before it was learned that terrorists were making a contact inside the swamp. One platoon established an ambush; one terrorist appeared and was killed. May passed without a contact. In June, a chance meeting by a patrol accounted for one killed and one captured. A few days later, after four fruitless days of patrolling, one platoon en route to camp accounted for two more terrorists. The Number 3 terrorist in the area surrendered and reported that food control was so effective that one terrorist had been murdered in a quarrel over food.

On July 7, two additional companies were assigned to the area; patrolling and harassing fires were intensified. Three terrorists surrendered and one of them led a platoon patrol to the terrorist leader's camp. The patrol attacked the camp, killing four, including the leader. Other patrols accounted for four more; by the end of July, twenty-three terrorists remained in the swamp with no food or communications with the outside world. . . .

This was the nature of operations: 60,000 artillery shells, 30,000 rounds of mortar ammunition, and 2,000 aircraft bombs for 35 terrorists killed or captured. Each one represented 1,500 man-days of patrolling or waiting in ambushes. "Nassau" was considered a success, for the end of the emergency was one step nearer.*

Nine months of continuous effort by an entire battalion, backed by artillery and aircraft, with the expenditure of more artillery and mortar shells and aerial bombs than exist in the arsenals of some Latin American republics—to eliminate *thirty-five* guerrillas.

*Marine Corps Schools, "Small Unit Operations," in *The Guerrilla—and How to Fight Him.*

At such cost, the defeat of the Chinese Communists in Malaya can be nothing less than inspirational to potential guerrillas of other, less sternly guarded countries. How many of the shaky Latin American regimes could meet the expense, let alone the political risks, of such a campaign, if it involved not thirty-five but a thousand determined guerrillas? For how long?

The British exchequer could, one supposes, conveniently stand the strain. Even so, there was more to the reckoning than the military payroll and the spectacular expenditure of ammunition. Undoubtedly the longdrawn MRLA insurrection, rootless and essentially hopeless as it was, hastened the independence of Malaya by some years.

*  *  *

We come to Greece—a case history of another sort. The three-year Greek revolution, successfully put down by a Rightest government with the help of Britain and the United States, offers instruction to those interested in knowing how *not* to conduct a guerrilla war.

In Greece (1946–49), virtually all of the lessons of experience were ignored, all of the rules laid down by the Marxist-Leninist theoreticians of revolutionary warfare were broken by the very Communists who might have been expected to adhere most closely to them.

As in other areas, the conclusion of World War II in Greece left the Communist leaders in an advantageous position, materially and politically. Communism and anti-fascism were closely identified because it was the Communists who had dominated the ELAS resistance movement; thus the Party held a strong ideological position. Thousands of ELAS veterans were at the disposal of the revolutionary movement. And although ELAS had made a token surrender of its weapons in 1945, the best of the arms supplied to the resistance groups by the British and Americans during the war remained in the hands of the guerrillas when civil war broke out in 1946.

Although the Communist guerrillas were numerically weak, with perhaps twenty-five hundred fighting men in 1946, as opposed to a national gendarmerie of 30,000, a good start was made, and recruits to the Communist cause poured in.

The fighting began in the northern mountains along Greece's common borders with Albania, Yugoslavia, and Bulgaria, soon spread to south-central Greece, and then into the mountains of the Peloponnesus. The reprisals taken by extreme right-wing groups added fuel to the flames, spreading the conflict.

The Communist campaign was initiated along theoretically sound lines. The Democratic Army fought in guerrilla fashion, in small units, capable of dispersing and hiding or even mingling with the civil population when in trouble, yet able to concentrate locally superior forces swiftly for attacks on village police posts and small patrols.

As the guerrillas grew stronger, the police were forced to abandon the smaller posts, and to withdraw for safety into the larger towns. The Athens government, seeing the danger, hastily began to rebuild the army, which had been reduced to virtually nothing during the German occupation.

The troops sent into the mountains to subdue the guerrillas encountered the same tactics. They were unable to hold small posts, unable to move freely except in considerable strength. Worse still, they were unable to maintain sufficient forces along the northern borders to prevent the passage of men and supply trains from Albania and Yugoslavia, where some four thousand ELAS veterans had gone when the German occupation had ended.

Thus the Democratic Army could depend on an inviolate rear area, across the border, in which to establish hospitals, training camps, and supply bases—the supplies moving into Greece by two main routes, one directly from Yugoslavia, the other from Yugoslavia to Albania and then southward.

The military strategy of the Greek guerrillas has been correctly defined as neither defensive nor offensive, but evasive. In short, it was the war of the flea: a nip here, a bite there, and a quick retreat. The object was to bleed the army, and through it the Athens government. Military objectives were subordinated to political goals: By cutting communications, sowing civil disorder, increasing the tax burden enormously, disrupting the economic life of the country, the Communists reasonably hoped to undermine the Athens regime and to create social, economic, and political pressures that would, in time, bring about its collapse.

In the field, the campaign went well—perhaps too well. The small bands of guerrillas grew rapidly; by early 1947 the Democratic Army was fighting in battalion strength, a year later brigades were formed, and then entire divisions—eight in all, organized roughly along the lines of conventional army divisions. The Democratic Army's initial strength had been about twenty-five hundred; at its peak, it reached twenty-six thousand, later declining to some eighteen thousand five hundred toward the end of the war.

Early success and other factors—the support given Athens by the British and then by the Americans, and that given the Democratic Army by the three Communist countries north of the border—led to serious, indeed fatal, errors.

The first was to lose effective contact with the Greek population. For reasons relating perhaps partly to political security, partly to simple material expedience, the Communists early in the campaign began to raid the villages from which the gendarmes had been driven and to strip them of their cattle, their food supplies, and eventually of their inhabitants—the latter being either forcibly inducted into the Democratic Army or driven out of the guerrilla base areas entirely.

Hordes of refugees from the war zones created something of a problem for Athens—but at heavy cost politically to the Communists, in terms of prestige and popular support throughout Greece. There were also military consequences: With a civil population in the war zones, the government had to think twice about bombing villages and scattered dwellings; civilians presented a serious problem of target identification to government pilots, who could not always know whether they were strafing a guerrilla mule supply train or a group of farmers on their way to market. With the war zones emptied of all but combatants, the bomber pilots as well as the troops on the ground had a free hand: Anything that moved, except government soldiers whose positions were known, was automatically a target.

The second major blunder of the Democratic Army, made for reasons till not entirely clear, was to begin in 1947 to try to hold ground, adopting conventional defensive tactics for which their inferior numbers, light arms, and weak logistical system were entirely unsuited.

The guerrillas had grown strong; eighteen thousand to twenty-six thousand men is a formidable force—for guerrillas. They were, however, obviously no match in any clear test of strength against an army and a National Defense Corps which together commanded some two hundred sixty-five thousand men, supported by armor, artillery, and a more than adequate air force.

Political considerations apparently entered into the Communist decision to attempt the transition from guerrilla warfare to more conventional operations: first the use of troops in brigade and divisional strength, then the attempt to hold ground in the north. A Communist government had been formed, and it required a territorial base. If world recognition was to be sought for a "Free Greece," it had to be demonstrated that such a Greece existed.

No doubt other factors bore on the decision. The Communists certainly needed, and in any case would have been reluctant to dispense with, their foreign bases and the supplies that came by mule train from Yugoslavia. To keep the borders open may have been one of the objects of the Democratic Army's defensive operations in the north.

Mistaken or not, the Democratic Army was at first successful in holding ground. In the summer of 1948, twelve thousand to fifteen thousand Communist troops held off fifty thousand government soldiers for two and a half months in the Grammos mountains, over an area of some two hundred square miles. When the pressure became too great, the Democratic Army withdrew into Albania, only to reappear in the Mount Vitsi region to the northeast, where a successful defense was made against renewed army operations. Within six months, the guerrillas had again established themselves in the Grammos. The government campaign in the north was, for the time being, defeated.

Defeat forced Athens to take drastic steps. General Alexander Papagos, former chief of the army general staff, was recalled from retirement and given what amounted to a free hand in reorganizing the army, with authority to raise its strength to a quarter of a million, if necessary.

Unsuitable officers were replaced by Papagos and new, aggressive tactics were adopted. Twenty-five thousand men were thrown into battle in the Peloponnesus, where the Communists had seized the offensive. By early 1949, the 3,600 guerrillas in that area had been liquidated, and the army was making good progress against those in central Greece. By the end of June, the Democratic Army had been defeated almost everywhere except in its Grammos and Mount Vitsi strongholds, and a strong offensive against these positions was in preparation.

The Communists, meanwhile, had been dealt a severe blow by the vagaries of international politics. Tito had fallen out with Stalin; Yugoslavia had left the Cominform; and in July the Belgrade government closed its border with Greece. Yugoslavia's action cut the guerrilla supply line into Macedonia and western Thrace, isolating some four thousand Communist reserves in Yugoslavia, and driving a wedge between the main force of Communists in the Grammos-Vitsi area and the guerrillas in Bulgaria, eastern Macedonia, and Thrace—some five thousand in all. The Democratic Army was still able to obtain some supplies from Albania, but far fewer and of poorer quality than had come from Yugoslavia.

Laboring against such difficulties, the Democratic Army proved unable long to resist better armed, better trained and organized regular troops in vastly superior numbers and with full artillery and air support. Within three days in August, the Mount Vitsi force of seven thousand was overrun, and five thousand guerrillas fled north into Albania. The government offensive in the Grammos lasted five days. By the time it was over, four thousand more guerrillas, the last remnants of the Democratic Army, had also withdrawn into Albania, and for all practical purposes the civil war in Greece was at an end.

Although thousands of erstwhile guerrillas and many more thousands of collaborators remained at large, scattered across the country, the revolution was destroyed beyond any hope of resurrection.

It seems not unfair to say that, to a very great extent, it was destroyed by the Communists themselves. Their alienation from the civil population in the northern mountains, the terrorism practiced against civilians, their dependence on foreign bases and supplies, and their premature decision in 1948 to hold ground and to expose large formations to a numerically, technologically, logistically, and organizationally superior army cost them a series of defeats from which there was no recovery.

Their loss was twofold. They were defeated militarily. And the Greek army's success spelled defeat for the revolutionary movement politically, as well.

\* \* \*

In the Greek context, the revolutionary principle bears repetition: The object of the guerrilla is not to win battles, but to avoid defeat, not to end the war, but to prolong it, until political victory, more important than any battlefield victory, has been won. In sacrificing the advantages of guerrilla tactics for military strategy based on territorial investment, the Greek Communists opposed strength with weakness. In risking a military confrontation, they gambled not only their available manpower, but something more important—their political prestige as a revolutionary force able to defy (by skillful evasion and superior tactics) the military colossus. And in losing the gamble, they lost the essential momentum, the high sense of popular anticipation, the bandwagon effect, on which the success of any political movement depends.

Revolution is by definition a mass phenomenon. Greece, Malaya, the Philippines all illustrate the axiom that without mass participation, or at least popular support, there can be no revolutions. The Huks lost it, the Chinese in Malaya never had it, the Greek Communists threw it away.

# SUN TZU ON THE ART OF WAR. PRINCIPLES OF GUERRILLA STRATEGY AND TACTICS. TERRAIN AS A DETERMINING FACTOR. GUERRILLA WAR IN URBAN AREAS. THE CHARACTER OF THE GUERRILLA.

All warfare is based on deception.

Therefore, when capable, feign incapacity; when active, inactivity.

When near, make it appear that you are far away; when far away, that you are near.

Offer the enemy a bait to lure him; feign disorder and strike him.

When he concentrates, prepare against him; where he is strong, avoid him.

Anger his general and confuse him.

Pretend inferiority and encourage his arrogance.

Keep him under a strain and wear him down.

When he is united, divide him.

Attack where he is unprepared; sally out when he does not expect you.

These are the strategist's keys to victory.

The quotation above is taken from Sun Tzu's essays on *The Art of War*, the oldest known writing on the subject, predating the Christian era by several centuries. The striking resemblance to the military axioms of Mao Tse-tung is no coincidence. Mao has studied Sun Tzu thoroughly and acknowledges his debt; many of the Chinese guerrilla leader's dicta are, in fact, mere paraphrases of those of *The Art of War*.

Sun Tzu is quoted here to make a point. It is that "modern warfare" is, in its most common usage, a cant phrase, indicative of the confusion of journalists and politicians who mistake technology for science. For despite the impressive technological innovations of the twentieth century, the principles of warfare are not modern but ancient; they were well established when Caesar marched out on his first campaign. And what is true of war in general is even more true, if possible, of guerrilla warfare in particular.

Aircraft and artillery provide weapons of far greater range than the longbow; explosives formidably multiply the striking power of the arrow; tanks are better than shields; trucks and helicopters offer (but not always) swifter and more dependable transportation than mules and camels. The problems of generalship remain the same. The variable factors of terrain, weather, space, time, population, and, above all, of morale and strategy still determine the outcome of battles and campaigns.

If there is anything new about guerrilla war—of which Sun Tzu surprisingly anticipates by two thousand years virtually all questions of a military nature—it is only in its modern, political application. To put it another way, the specifically modern aspect of guerrilla warfare is in its use as a tool of political revolution—the single sure method by which an unarmed population can overcome mechanized armies, or, failing to overcome them, can stalemate them and make them irrelevant.

To understand how this comes about does not require a study of military tactics so much as of the political problems to which military methods—guerrilla methods—may provide a solution.

The guerrilla is a political insurgent, the conscious agent of revolution; his military role, while vital, is only incidental to his political mission. His insurgency is dedicated to a single purpose: the overthrow of the government and the destruction of the existing political or social or, it may be, economic system.

In the process of accomplishing his goal, he may have to defeat—and he will certainly have to engage and out-maneuver—organized, professional military forces. If so, however, his maneuvers, except where immediate survival is at stake, will be undertaken primarily for their political effect. Each battle will be a lesson, designed to demonstrate the impotence of the army and so to discredit the government that employs it. Each campaign will be a text, intended to raise the level of revolutionary awareness and anticipation of the popular majority whose attitude will determine the outcome of the struggle.

Guerrilla actions will have certain obvious military objectives: to obtain weapons, ammunition, and supplies, to inflict casualties, to force the enemy to overextend his lines so that his communications may be disrupted and small units picked off, one at a time, by locally superior rebel forces.

But psychological and political objectives will be paramount. Local military success will serve no purpose if the guerrilla campaign does not also weaken the morale of the government and its soldiers, strain the financial resources of the regime, and increase political pressure on it by creating widespread apprehension and dissatisfaction with the progress of a war in which there is no progress—and no end in sight.

Obviously, none of this can occur except in the presence of certain distinct social and political conditions, which combine to produce a potentially revolutionary situation. Successful insurgency presupposes the existence of valid popular grievances, sharp social divisions, an unsound or stagnant economy, an oppressive government. These factors obtaining, revolution will still be far off, unless there exists or comes into existence the nucleus of a revolutionary organization, capable of articulating and exploiting popular dissatisfaction with the *status quo.*

Ordinarily, however, revolutionary situations produce their own revolutionary leadership. Coming from the most unstable social sectors, it can be expected to include the most radical, most frustrated and ambitious elements of the political "out" parties, the more idealistic and least successful members of the middle class, and those most outraged by the *unaccustomed* pinch of oppression. (The long-tyrannized peasant, for example, is seldom as revolutionary as the relatively fortunate student or worker who has been led to believe that he has rights, and finds, in a change of political climate, that he is deprived of them.)

In the potentially revolutionary situation, spontaneous insurrections may be expected: They are likely to arise out of almost any sort of social conflict—a strike, an election campaign, a dispute over land or wages or prices or rents or schools or any one of a score of other social "problems." Often they will come in reaction to some act of repression or of real or fancied injustice on the part of the governing authorities as, for example, when the efforts of the police to curb a popular demonstration turn the demonstration into a riot.

In other circumstances, disorder may be deliberately created. In Cuba, Algeria, Cyprus, as examples that come readily to mind, the war of the flea was initiated by the deliberate acts of the revolutionary nucleus, proclaiming its defiance of authority and banking on popular support in an open declaration of revolutionary war.

The means are not important. The important element is the leadership itself. Bandits are not revolutionaries, looters are not guerrillas. In order to attract a following, the revolutionary leaders must stand on firm moral ground; they must have some greater purpose than the furtherance of personal ambition. This in turn implies an ideology or a clear "cause" to explain their decisions and the reasons of their insurgency. They cannot be mere opportunists.

When conflict occurs, whether spontaneous or induced, the revolutionary leaders must be capable of explaining and rationalizing its confused and often apparently accidental character. Isolated acts of defiance must be given coherency within a revolutionary frame of reference. The leadership must be prepared to make the most of every opportunity to accelerate the process of social ferment and political disruption. The first task of the revolutionary cadres must be to relate each incident and each phase of the conflict to a great "cause," so that revolutionary violence is seen as the natural and moral means to a desired end, and the masses of the people are increasingly involved. The struggle cannot be allowed to seem meaningless or chaotic. It must be given a progressive character in all its phases; it must arouse great expectations and appear crucial at every stage, so that no one can stand outside of it.

The precise "cause" itself is not of great consequence: One is often as good as another. In Cuba, for example, the corruption of the Batista regime and its illegitimacy were seemingly sufficient "causes" for the well-to-do middle class—so long as its members individually did not take any great personal risk, but merely sympathized with and abetted the active revolutionaries. When the sons of the middle class were imprisoned or killed or tortured for their activities, oppression became the more urgent "cause."

Economic nationalism was the real "cause" of the rich and ambitious industrialists and entrepreneurs who opposed Batista. Political ambition, which could not be avowed, and a sense of social injustice, which could, were the "causes" that drove the frustrated youths of the poor white-collar class to become the cadres and greatest zealots of the revolution. And on the other hand, the landless *campesinos*, the economically deprived *macheteros* of the great sugar plantations, the squatters of the Sierra Maestra were driven by actual hunger, by real oppression, and by a longing for the security of land of their own under a just social system—motivations that transcended any question of moral or political "causes."

The nominal causes varied according to the local situation. The constant, consistent appeal of the revolutionary leadership was broader, being based on a democratic, egalitarian ideology linked to notions of social justice long accepted in Cuba (there was nothing new about Castro's brand of "humanism," it was written into the Cuban constitution), and a clear political goal—the overthrow of the Batista regime and the complete destruction of or severance from everything that supported it.

The overthrow of Batista was presented as a panacea, the remedy of all existing evils. As a "cause," it related and made understandable each isolated political development: the assassination of a policeman, the martyrdom of a terrorist, the suspension of civil liberties or a public demonstration demanding their restoration, any disruption of the ordinary routine, anything that helped to undermine the regime, was held up as a skirmish or a battle in a great crusade.

This state of mind prevailing, the process of cutting away Batista's support and increasing the pressure against him both inside and outside of the country continued according to a pattern that we have already examined in detail in earlier chapters.

The Cuban example provides as well as any other the recipe for successful insurgency. The prerequisites are the following:

1. An unstable political situation, marked by sharp social divisions and usually, but not always, by a foundering or stagnant economy.

2. A political objective, based on firm moral and ideological grounds, that can be understood and accepted by the majority as the overriding "cause" of the insurgency, desirable in itself and worthy of any sacrifice.

3. An oppressive government, with which no political compromise is possible.

4. Some form of revolutionary political organization, capable of providing dedicated and consistent leadership toward the accepted goal.

There is one final requirement: the clear possibility or even the probability of success. Until people believe that a government *can* be overthrown—and it must be the first act of the insurgency to demonstrate this possibility by successful defiance of military force—the attempt will not be made, the revolutionary following will not be found.

The specific techniques or tactics of guerrilla warfare are not, except in unimportant detail, to be learned from texts. They relate always to the specific local situation and are supremely expedient: The guerrilla is, above all, an improviser. The nature of his improvisation depends, naturally, on immediate and long-range objectives, the terrain, the relative strength of his forces and those of the enemy, the material means at his disposal, and similar factors.

Since the guerrilla's numerical strength and arms are inferior to those of his enemy (or he would not be a guerrilla), and since his most immediate concern is mere survival, the basis of all guerrilla tactics is, obviously, evasion. Successful evasion means the ability to avoid confrontation except at one's own choosing

yet always to be able to achieve the *local* superiority to strike
with effect.

"If I am able to determine the enemy's disposition while at
the same time I conceal my own," writes Sun Tzu, "then I can
concentrate and he must divide. And if I concentrate while he
divides, I can use my entire strength to attack a fraction of his."

And again:

"The enemy must not know where I intend to give battle. For
if he does not know where I intend to give battle, he must prepare in a great many places. And when he prepares in a great
many places, those I have to fight in any one place will be few.
. . . *And when he prepares everywhere, he will be weak everywhere.*"

The foregoing explains, as well as anything that has ever been
written, how it is possible for a relative handful of armed men
to oppose a vastly superior army. The secrets of success are, first,
superior intelligence, and, second, terrain. Guerrillas, representing a popular cause, have the tremendous advantage of an intelligence service that encompasses virtually the entire population.
The population hides them, and at the same time it reveals, from
day to day and hour to hour, the disposition and strength of the
enemy.

"We always know where the soldiers are," Fidel Castro told
me when I first interviewed him in the Sierra Maestra, early in
1957, "but they never know where we are. We can come and go
as we like, moving through their lines, but they can never find
us unless we wish them to, and then it is only on our terms."*

At the time, Castro had perhaps one hundred guerrillas at his
disposal; in theory, he was "surrounded" by some five thousand
Batista soldiers. But in the wild and trackless terrain of the Sierra
Maestra, roaming over some five thousand square miles of
mountains and dense forest among the rural populace surely
sympathetic to him and hostile to Batista, his being "surrounded" was an irrelevance. The ocean is surrounded, but the
fish do not care.

Where a choice of ground is possible, the terrain for guerrilla
operations should be carefully selected. The ideal will be found

---

*Robert Taber: *M—26: The Biography of a Revolution.*

in a country that is more rural than urban, mountainous rather than flat, thickly forested rather than bare, with extensive railway lines, bad roads, and an economy that is preponderantly agricultural rather than industrial. The relative dispersion or concentration of the population is also of great importance: A region with a widely scattered rural population, living in small hamlets and isolated farm dwellings is much more vulnerable than one of tightly knit, large country towns separated by wide areas of open farmland.

The terrain should afford both natural concealment and obstacles to hinder the movement of military transport—mountains and swamps where tanks and trucks cannot go, woods and thick brush that provide cover from aerial observation and attack, forests from which to strike quickly and safely at enemy rail and highway communications and in which to ambush small military units.

There should be sufficient space to maneuver freely, without the danger of being caught in a closing spiral of encirclement. The greater the area of operations, the more difficult it will be for the army to locate the guerrillas and the more the government will have to disperse its troops and extend its line of supply and communication.

Yet the guerrillas cannot choose the remotest and most rugged areas in which they would be safest. They must remain constantly in contact with the rural population from which to recruit, to draw supplies, and to obtain reliable couriers who will carry messages and directions to and from the revolutionary underground in the towns and cities.

This necessity indicates the choice of an area with a dispersed rather than concentrated rural population. Such an area will usually afford the natural concealment and natural obstacles to army operations found in desolate areas, and will provide a further advantage: It will not be economic for the government to garrison.

Large rural towns can be garrisoned; tiny hamlets cannot. Where there are many of them, only a few soldiers can be assigned to each, and to create such rural outposts is worse than useless, since each individual post can easily be overwhelmed, its soldiers captured or killed, their arms and ammunition seized, and another propaganda victory thus scored by the insurgents.

Since there will be no great government stake in any given hamlet, farm, or village, in economic or strategic terms, the natural decision of the army will be to withdraw to safer ground. Yet each such withdrawal will widen the area of guerrilla control and feed the insurgency, providing it with more supplies, more recruits, more room in which to maneuver.

There is another consideration: The possession of populated areas will usually provide almost as much safety for the insurgents as would the remote areas in which they cannot be located or attacked. Political considerations, if not those of humanity, will usually offer some safeguard against bombing or artillery attacks, since the government cannot afford to kill civilians indiscriminately.*

The danger of being isolated far from populated areas has been demonstrated by the experience of guerrillas in Malaya and the Philippines. In both instances, the military succeeded in isolating the insurgents, cutting them off from the source of their strength, with results fatal to the insurgency. On the other hand, the possibility of fighting a successful guerrilla war on a small island with little room to maneuver and no real wilderness sanctuary has been proven by the Cypriot fighters of EOKA. When pressed, the small guerrilla bands commanded by Grivas in the hills of Cyprus would filter back into the towns. The known fugitives who could not do so lived like foxes in earthen dugouts, so well camouflaged that British soldiers often walked above their heads without discovering them. Others allied forth on night forays from hiding places under the floors of homes where they had lain all day, their presence unsuspected. They were, in the most literal sense, "underground."

Even in well policed, large cities, a sympathetic population can protect active insurgents. The draconian methods used by the French in Algiers virtually stamped out the F.L.N. underground there, but only because the Moslems of the Casbah were

---

*Clearly this does not always hold. Consider Viet Nam.

already separated, racially and physically, from the French population. Soldiers, especially foreigners, can suppress urban rebellion (as in Budapest) by treating the entire metropolis as a city under wartime siege, controlling all movements, and ruthlessly killing the inhabitants of any quarter where resistance is offered. Gradually an urban popoulation can be starved and terrorized into submission. But such methods scarcely apply to the civil war situation in which there is no sure way of knowing friend from foe.

Terrain and local conditions ultimately decide the size and organization of the guerrilla band. In Cuba's Sierra Maestra, "columns" of one hundred to one hundred twenty men proved best, such a force being competent to deal with any military group that might penetrate its base area. Greater numbers were unwieldy on the march and difficult to supply, given the resources of a very thinly populated region with a marginal agricultural economy.

In more densely populated, more prosperous rural areas, a platoon of thirty to forty men would occupy a hamlet or small village and its environs; guard posts were established along the margins of the entire "territorio libre," and the zone was administered as a state within a state.

In suburban areas, on the other hand, concealment was the determining factor, and the guerrillas who worked close to the larger towns, interdicting the highways and cutting communications and power lines, operated in squads of three to eight men, striking from ambush and then quickly hiding in the brush or, at times, in the homes of residents. Raids on suburban military posts and outlying industrial establishments were often made by commandos living within the town, who would assemble for a night action and then quickly disperse to their homes, to resume their normal daytime occupations.

With respect to the conditions that prevail in most of the Latin American republics, Che Guevara considers that a nucleus of *thirty to fifty* armed men is sufficient to initiate a guerrilla insurgency with good assurance of success. If the nucleus, organized and armed in strictest secrecy, exceeds one hundred fifty, it should be divided, and the action begun in two regions well apart. When an active guerrilla column grows beyond one hundred or so, it should again be divided, and action begun on a new front. There is a positive as well as a negative reason for this division: The guerrillas are missionaries; their task is not merely to oppose the army but to spread rebellion among the people; and the wider their area of contact with the population, the better for their cause.

The guerrilla nucleus initiates the conflict, if possible, on the edge of a wilderness sanctuary, in a thinly populated agricultural area with a marginal economy, within easy striking distance of strategic targets—railway lines that can be cut, communications that can be disrupted, mining or industrial plants that can be sabotaged, small military or police posts from which arms can be seized. At the same time, urban insurrection of a hit-and-run rather than sustained character is created by the revolutionary underground, so as to give the insurgency a general, national complexion for maximum propaganda effect. It is not enough to rebel: The rebellion must be the object of national attention, too shocking in its initial effects to be ignored by even a controlled press, or quickly explained away, as has been the case with many abortive provincial insurrections, by a government safe in an untroubled capital, far from the scene of battle.

When the first excitement has died away and order has been restored in the towns where uprisings have occurred, the guerrillas can expect the army to bring the battle to them; they will not have to seek it. The government will order a "bandit suppression" campaign. Troops will be dispatched by motor convoy or airlift to the region of reported guerrilla activity; spotter planes will skim the treetops seeking the insurgents; soldiers will occupy the villages and patrol the roads; foot columns will penetrate deeply into rebel territory, trying to make contact. Helicopters may be used to ferry troops to strategic encampments deep in the forest or mountains from which patrols can fan out in search of the rebels. If the military commander knows what he is about, he may adopt some variation of the French "oil slick" technique, gridding the region on his map and attempting to clear it a square at a time, driving the guerrillas slowly toward a prepared "killing zone" (or zones) where their only apparent route of escape will bring them into the open—much as tigers are driven by beaters into the guns of the hunters.

The "oil slick" method is theoretically sound, but in practice it is far from foolproof. Since it is a rare government that can admit serious concern over the activities of a small band of guerrillas, the chances are that the military force sent on the suppression campaign will be far from adequate for a task in which a ratio of ten to one is prescribed and five hundred soldiers to each guerrilla would not be at all excessive.*

Regardless of the number of troops involved, the guerrillas will fight according to certain principles. They will not seek to hold ground or to contend with a stronger force, but only to confuse and exhaust it and to inflict casualties on it, without taking casualties in return. The key to this kind of action is the well placed ambush. "Generally," writes Sam Tzu, "he who occupies the field of battle first and awaits his enemy is at ease; he who comes later to the fight and rushes into battle is weary."

The guerrillas will not give battle until the terrain favors them. Their effort will be to lure the enemy into situations in which numbers are of little account, because the way is too steep and the passage too narrow for more than a few to proceed at a time. When fighting begins, it will be on ground of the rebels' own choosing—preferably from commanding heights with dense cover and limited visibility, where a few determined men can hold up an army.

Ambushes will be prepared in such a manner that a small portion of the advancing military column—its vanguard—will be separated from the rest when firing commences. The fire of the main body of the guerrillas will be concentrated on this vanguard. The object of the ambush must be the complete destruc-

*In Cuba, in 1961, more than 60,000 Castro militia were used to suppress an insurgency in the Escambray mountains, supplied by CIA airdrops, involving not more than 600 anti-Castro guerrillas with little or no popular support. The ratio of troops to insurgents was thus 100 to 1 or better; the cleanup nevertheless required nearly three months to accomplish.

This is not heresay; the author was there.

tion of the advance group and seizure of its arms and ammunition, the latter task being accomplished while a small guerrilla rear guard delays the rest of the military column.

In this connection, Che Guevara writes:

> When the force of the guerrilla band is small and it is desired above all to detain and slow down the advance of an invading column, groups of snipers, from two to ten in number, should be distributed all around the column at each of the four cardinal points. In this situation, combat can be begun, for example, on the right flank; when the enemy centers his action on that flank and fires on it, shooting will begin at that moment from the left flank; at another moment from the rear guard or from the vanguard, and so forth.
>
> With a very small expenditure of ammunition it is possible to hold the enemy in check indefinitely.

While the column is delayed, the main body of the guerrilla force quickly gathers its military booty and moves on toward the next prepared position, or circles around and steps out in a new direction. The snipers withdraw and rejoin the main force before the troops have recovered sufficiently to launch a counterattack, all of this occurring within a matter of a few minutes.

The process is repeated again and again. When it has been determined that a military column is sufficiently isolated that the arrival of reinforcements can be delayed for some hours or days, the guerrillas may even attempt an encirclement, or may create the appearance of an encirclement by stationing squads of snipers on commanding ground in such a way as to bring the troops under fire in whichever direction they attempt to move. If the troops launch a determined assault, the guerrillas have only to give way, circle around, regroup, and again withdraw.

The superior mobility and small size of the guerrilla force are its main assets. The danger that they themselves may be encircled is usually more apparent than real.

Night, as Guevara has noted, is the best ally of the guerrilla fighter. Although the Cubans used the phrase, "encirclement face," to describe the look of someone who was frightened, Castro's guerrillas never suffered a single casualty through encirclement, and Guevara considers it no real problem for a guerrilla force. His prescription: Take adequate measures to impede the advance of the enemy until nightfall and then exfiltrate—a relatively simple matter for a small group of men in country well known to them, where the cover is good.

In the first months of the insurgency, when the army is on the offensive, the tactics of ambush and evasion are standard and sufficient. The activities of the army itself are enough to advertise the rebel cause. Mounting military casualties cannot be kept secret. The high cost of the anti-guerrilla campaign will be an embarrassment to the government, which will be hard put to explain what it is doing—and failing to do. And each encounter will strengthen the guerrillas while weakening the morale of their military opponents.

"The guerrilla soldier ought always to have in mind," writes Guevara, "that his source of supply of arms is the enemy and that, except in special circumstances, he ought not to engage in a battle that will not lead to the capture of such equipment."

The enemy vanguard is made a special target of guerrilla fire for a sound psychological reason: to induce the fear, or at any rate the excessive caution, that will paralyze the will and retard the free movement of the enemy. When the soldiers in the first rank invariably are killed, few will wish to be in the vanguard, and without a vanguard there is no movement. (Such reasoning may not always apply to professional troops. Professional officers are trained to accept casualties as the price of battle. Nevertheless it has been a constant complaint of American military advisers in South Viet Nam that the Vietnamese field commanders commonly refuse to advance against strong guerrilla positions without artillery support and preparatory air strikes that give the Viet Cong guerrillas time to retire from the field.)

The insurgency continuing, the military may be expected sooner or later to give up the futile pursuit of the guerrilla force and leave it to its wilderness sanctuary, if for no other reason than the political. As has been remarked before, few governments can long sustain the political embarrassment of an expensive and well-publicized campaign in which there is no progress to report. Within a matter of weeks or months, the government will be forced to announce a victory, having failed to produce one. The public outside of the war zone will be informed that the insurrection has been suppressed, the bodies of a few civilian casualties may even be displayed by way of evidence, and the troops will be withdrawn to posts and garrisons in more settled territory, falling back on a strategy of *containment* of the insurrection.

If the insurgency is to succeed, the guerrillas must, of course, refuse to be contained. They will now assume the offensive, taking advantage of their new freedom to organize night raids on the small military outposts that ring their free zone, and using the attacks on such outposts as bait to lure military reinforcements into ambush on the roads.

As successful action provides more arms, new guerrilla units are organized, and new zones of operations opened. Guerrillas filtering through the army lines attack isolated military and police units in the villages on the periphery of their free zone, forcing the army to pull back to reinforce these points. With still more room in which to maneuver, rebels occupy the outlying farms, move into small hamlets that cannot be defended economically. Efforts will now be made to discourage, although not absolutely to prevent, military convoys from entering certain zones. The roads will be mined, tank traps dug, defenses in depth constructed so that the troops will have to fight their way into rebel territory through a series of ambuscades, the guerrillas at each stage offering light resistance and then falling back on the next position.

As rebel strength grows, the army is confronted with a difficult dilemma. Having superior numbers and heavier arms, it will still be able to enter the rebel zones in strength, but only at the cost of some casualties, and with no advantage, since the ground gained will have no strategic or economic value commensurate with the cost of occupying it. If the troops should remain in force, the guerrillas would simply transfer their operations to another zone: The army cannot be everywhere. Yet if the troops do *not* remain, the territory is, in effect, ceded to the insurgents, who proceed to turn its agricultural economy and its rural population to their own purpose. This is the dilemma of the military commander.

It is, of course, sharpened by political problems. Large chunks of the agricultural economy cannot be surrendered to the insurgents without political consequences. Those whose fortunes are affected—traders, absentee landowners, and the like—will be certain to put pressure on the government to *do* something. They may seek political alternatives. The general public will be excited and divided by the deterioration of the government's position, as it becomes more apparent. The more radical elements of urban society will be emboldened; revolutionary sentiment, stirred up by the underground, will grow stronger and more widespread, and the government will grow progressively more fearful and repressive.

In such circumstances, and considering that no army can occupy *all* of the national territory, the logical and natural course of the regime will be the gradual withdrawal of troops from the countryside to the larger centers of population. The rural areas thus will be slowly and reluctantly surrendered to the insurgents. With expanded resources of manpower and material, the insurgency will continue to grow. As it gains strength, guerrilla bands will become guerrilla armies. The larger villages will be captured. The railway bridges will be blown and the highways cut. One by one the towns and then the cities will be isolated, their vital supplies restricted, civilian transport reduced to a trickle. Military convoys may still come and go, but not without peril, and not with any important effect, in a country most of which will already be in the hands of the revolution.

The pattern described above is observable. It has already happened in the Western Hemisphere; it is happening right now in Southeast Asia.

Certainly it is not the only pattern that revolutionary warfare can follow. Is the United States itself immune? The complexity of modern, urban, heavily industrialized societies makes them extremely vulnerable to wide-scale sabotage, a fact that has not gone unremarked by the extremists of the small but fanatical Black Nationalist movement in the United States. The extent of their commitment may be judged by the February, 1965, disclosure of a bizarre plot, said to have been hatched by members of the Black Nationalist Revolutionary Action Movement, to blow up the Statue of Liberty in New York, the Liberty Bell in Philadelphia, and the Washington Monument. In an article in Esquire published just four months earlier (October, 1964) entitled "The Red Chinese American Negro," the Negro journalist William Worthy reported:

> With an eye on expected financial and material support from Asia and Africa, RAM has proclaimed the necessity to utilize "the three basic principal powers" held by Negroes:
> "1. The power to stop the machinery of government.
> "2. The power to hurt the economy.
> "3. The power of unleashing violence."

The details were clearly spelled out elsewhere by a Negro leader who has since been linked to RAM. Writing in the monthly newsletter, *The Crusader*, Robert William, a former chapter president of the National Association for the Advancement of Colored People who fled to Cuba after a racial incident in Monroe, North Carolina, in 1961, pictured the coming black revolution in the United States in the following terms:

> When massive violence comes, the U.S.A. will become a bedlam of confusion and chaos. . . . The factory . . . telephone . . . and radio workers will be afraid to report to their jobs. All transportation will grind to a complete standstill. . . . Essential pipelines will be severed and blown up and all manner of sabotage will occur. . . . A clash will occur inside the Army Forces. At U.S. military bases around the world local revolutionaries will side with Afro G.I.'s. . . .
> The new concept of revolution defies military science and tactics. The new concept is lightning campaigns conducted in highly sensitive urban communities, with the paralysis reaching the small communities and spreading to the farm areas. The old method of guerrilla warfare, as carried out from the hills and countryside, would be ineffective in a powerful country like the U.S.A. Any such force would be wiped out in an hour.

The new concept is to huddle as close to the enemy as possible so as to neutralize his modern and fierce weapons. The new concept . . . dislocates the organs of harmony and order and reduces central power to the level of a helpless, sprawling octopus. During the hours of day sporadic rioting takes place and massive sniping. Night brings all-out warfare, organized fighting, and unlimited terror against the oppressor and his forces. Such a campaign will bring about an end to oppression and social injustice in the U.S.A. in less than ninety days. . . .

Williams quotes from an interview which he claims to have had with one "Mr. Lumumba" (a pseudonym adopted in honor of the murdered Congolese premier, Patrice Lumumba), a purported underground leader with a plan for guerrilla warfare in the United States:

The United States is very vulnerable, economically and physically.

Black youth with the right orientation can stop this entire country. Small bands can damage the eight major dams that supply most of the electricity. Electricity means mass communications.

Gasoline can be poured into the sewer systems in major urban areas and then ignited. This would burn out communications lines in an entire city.

What would emerge from this chaos? Most likely, guerrilla warfare. I don't think the entire white community will fight. . . . But the entire black community will be fighting.

We call the whites "cream puffs." We feel that when TV stops, when the telephone no longer rings, their world will almost come to an end. Like during a major air raid, they will stay in the house. They'll sit and wait for television to come on.

There is much exaggeration in all of this, and some pure, ranting demagoguery, along with what may well be an honest misappraisal of the situation. As yet, there is no evidence that the Negro minority in the United States is prepared for or disposed to violence—or, indeed, finds adequate cause. Yet the Black Nationalists have a point: Where the will to resist authority exists on a wide scale, the means can be found; nor are urban, industrial societies, however well policed, guerrilla-proof.

The guerrilla succeeds because he survives. He flourishes because his methods are progressive. With a pistol, a machete, or, for that matter, a bow and arrow, he can capture a rifle. With twenty rifles he can capture a machine gun, and with twenty rifles and a machine gun he can capture a military patrol or destroy a convoy that carries five machine guns and fifty thousand rounds of ammunition. With a dozen shovels and a few gallons of gasoline he can destroy a tank, and with its weapons he can shoot down an airplane or a helicopter that also carries weapons.

Artillery is useless against him because it never catches up with him. A five-hundred-pound aerial bomb will dig a crater ten feet deep and fifteen feet wide, but it will not disturb a guerrilla in a slit trench ten yards away. A dozen aircraft dropping napalm can splash liquid fire over a hundred acres of woodland, but it will have no effect unless the guerrillas happen to be in that hundred acres, out of the thousands through which they roam.

Once the war of the flea has reached settled rural regions, even these limited means become ineffective, because aircraft cannot attack guerrillas without killing the civilians whose support the government must win—and they all look alike from the air. Great faith was placed in helicopters; they were of service in the Sahara but have failed to come up to expectations in the jungles of Viet Nam, where the Viet Cong has learned to set successful traps for them and crew casualties are heavy.

United States military handbooks on irregular warfare techniques discuss various biological and chemical weapons that can be employed against guerrillas. These are recommended especially for situations in which guerrillas have mingled with an innocent civilian population that cannot—or ought not—to be killed.

The object of the so-called biologicals is to induce temporarily incapacitating viral diseases that will reduce the ability of guerrillas to resist attack, so that infantry can rush into a target area and quickly kill or capture them without harming noncombatants—a device, so to speak, for separating the sheep from the goats.

Various nonlethal gases—carried, like the biologicals, in artillery shells or aerial bombs, or sprayed by low-flying planes or helicopters—have been designed for the same purpose, to sicken all within a given target area and so reduce resistance to infantrymen on their arrival, without unnecessary bloodshed.

The concept is certainly humane and logical. In practice it has proved faulty. On the three occasions in which nonlethal gas (a mixture of vomiting gas and tear gas, of the type used to control rioters) was used in South Viet Nam during early 1965, the practical results were nil. Twice the gas simply blew away, without any effect. On the third occasion, it sickened a few residents of the target area, but the infantrymen who soon arrived found no guerrillas in the area.

The propaganda effects, on the other hand, were tremendous—and adverse in the extreme. When Washingon casually announced in March, 1965, that *gas* has been used in Viet Nam, the political repercussions were heard around the world within twenty-four hours. The Asian press—especially the Japanese, forever scarred by the Horishima and Nagasaki bombs—was loud in indignation. London and Paris made diplomatic inquiries. And much of the United States press itself sternly condemned the use of even the most harmless gas as a serious breach of all civilized conventions of warfare, that could lead to who knew what barbarity.

Considering the great effect of the Chinese charges of "germ warfare" against the Americans during the Korean war, and the fresh outcry against gas, it is doubtful that guerrillas will have much to fear from either gas or biological warfare in the near future, especially since the practical military value remains unproven. Other weapons of modern military technology are more frightening. White phosphorous is invariably crippling if not fatal because it burns through to the bone; it will penetrate steel, and nothing extinguishes it but total immersion.

A new, one-thousand-pound parcel bomb opens in the air to strew a hundred anti-personnel bombs over as many yards—a weapon far more effective against guerrillas than the concentrated detonation of a single high-explosive missile.

New amphibious gun carriers can penetrate the deepest swamps and marshes. Infra-red and heat-sensitive sniperscopes detect guerrillas in the dark. A later model operates by magnifying the light of the stars. Mobile radar units can spot infiltraters on the ground at a thousand yards. Silent weapons make the trained guerrilla-hunter patrol even harder to detect than guerrillas themselves.

Yet when all is said and done, even the counterinsurgency experts admit that technology alone can never defeat guerrillas: It can only make their task more difficult and dangerous.

The crux of the struggle is the social and political climate. The flea survives by hopping and hiding; he prevails because he multiplies far faster than he can be caught and exterminated.

\* \* \*

The needs of the guerrilla are few: his rifle, a blanket, a square of some impermeable material to shelter him from the rain, a knife, a compass, stout boots—the minimum of ordinary camping equipment. Personal qualifications are greater. Physically, the guerrilla must be strong, with iron legs and sound lungs; temperamentally, he must be a cheerful stoic and an ascetic; he must like the hard life he leads. But what is indispensable is ideological armor. Above all, the revolutionary activist must stand on solid moral ground, if he is to be more than a political bandit.

One is led to believe, as in the case of the Viet Cong, for example, that guerrillas dominate unprotected rural people by threats and terror: It is a convenient thing for country people to say when confronted by government soldiers who ask them why they have sheltered guerrillas.

In general, it is not true. There are judicious uses of terror, no doubt, but no guerrilla can afford to use it against the people on whose support and confidence he depends for his life as well as for his political existence. People are quick to detect the difference between opportunism and dedication, and it is the latter that they respect and follow.

To be successful, the guerrilla must be loved and admired. To attract followers, he must represent not merely success, but absolute virtue, so that his enemy will represent absolute evil. If the soldiers are idle, drunken, and licentious, the guerrilla must be vigorous, sober, and moral. If enemies are to be disposed of, it must be for moral reasons: They must be traitors, murderers, rapists. The revolution must show that its justice is sure and swift. By contrast, its enemies must be revealed as venal, weak, and vacillating.

The successful guerrilla leader must be fair in his dealings, paying for the goods he takes, and respecting personal property and individual rights, even those of persons not partisan to his cause, in the realization that the society in which he works is an intricate and interlocking machinery and that he requires all the support he can get. Even where the war is at bottom a class struggle—and this is not always the case—class rivalries should be softened rather than sharpened, subordinated to a transcendental, national cause. Those in doubt, even the adherents and servants of the regime, must be given a clear moral choice. They must be told, in effect: It is still not too late to join forces with virtue, and to have a share in the bright future, more secure and certain than the property or the position you value now.

Revolutionary propaganda must be essentially *true* in order to be believed. This is simple expedience. If it is not believed, people cannot be induced to act on it, and there will be no revolution. Guerrilla leaders do not inspire the spirit of sacrifice and revolutionary will that creates popular insurrection by promises alone, or by guns alone. A high degree of selfless dedication and high purpose is required. Whether the primary cause of revolution is nationalism, or social justice, or the anticipation of material progress, the decision to fight and to sacrifice is a social and a moral decision. Insurgency is thus a matter not of manipulation but of inspiration.

I am aware that such conclusions are not compatible with the picture of guerrilla operations and guerrilla motivation drawn by the counterinsurgency theorists who are so much in vogue today. But the counterinsurgency experts have yet to win a war. At this writing, they are certainly losing one.

Their picture is distorted because their premises are false and their observation faulty. They assume—perhaps their commitments require them to assume—that politics is mainly a manipulative science and insurgency mainly a politico-military technique to be countered by some other technique; whereas both are forms of social behavior, the latter being the mode of popular resistance to unpopular governments.

# GUERRILLA MOVEMENTS IN THE THIRD WORLD. THE REVOLUTIONARY BASE. OUTLOOK FOR THE UNITED STATES. PROPOSALS FOR A NEW AMERICAN FOREIGN POLICY IN LATIN AMERICA.

In the consideration of the various historical, theoretical, and practical aspects of guerrilla warfare, two things become clear.

The first is that the war of the flea, as it is seen today, is not merely popular war, but the war of the world's *have-nots*, the natural weapon lending itself to the situation of subjugated and exploited peoples everywhere. In short, it is a revolutionary weapon.

The second is that the United States, by reason of its position of commanding wealth and power, is cast—like it or not—in a counterrevolutionary role. As the world's greatest economic and military power, greatest banker, financier, investor, mercantilist, industrialist, and principal practitioner and guardian of the system of capitalistic free enterprise (of which liberal democracy and constitutional government are considered to be part and parcel), the United States is naturally and necessarily allied with bankers, landlords, and investors everywhere. Despite American tradition and cant, American foreign policy, favoring the peaceful *status quo* and quiet social evolution as against radical revolution, is anti-popular wherever popular movements run counter to vested economic interest. If at times we seem to oppose vested interest, it is hard to avoid the conclusion that it is expediently in favor of greater economic opportunity—ours.

Cold War considerations stiffen this position. On the one hand, the United States opposes Communism in defense of property and free enterprise; on the other, it opposes it as the agency of Soviet or of Chinese expansionism, viewing the Chinese and the Russian blocs both as rival politico-economic systems and as potential military threats.

Since most of the revolutionary movements now arising in the world are, if not Communist by definition or Marxist-Leninist in ideology, at least socialistically inclined (hence apparent threats to the enterprise system) it is not surprising to find the United States in opposition to them—Viet Nam and the Congo being the prime examples of the moment. Even where the revolutionary objective is not socialism, but merely a position of economic independence and of political nonalignment, the United States, seeking to secure its investments and to expand its influence and markets, scarcely welcomes revolution.*

The result: United States interest and policy versus the rising revolution of the submerged masses of the underdeveloped areas of the world. The logical development of the situation suggests further extensions of what is now occurring in South Viet Nam: the confrontation of American wealth, influence, industrial power, and in the show-down, American arms, with guerrilla movements in every major area of United States interest.

The study of guerrilla movements of the postwar era leads to the conclusion that the United States is slowly moving into a worldwide conflict which it cannot win.

The reasons are not mysterious.

As we have seen, guerrilla war is popular war in one form or another. It is the struggle of nations against foreign invaders, or rebellious segments of a society against the ruling classes of that society, of exploited against exploiters, of the governed against the governors.

In Cyprus, as an example that we have already examined, a

---

*Washington's attitude is nowhere more strikingly demonstrated than in the recent armed intervention in the Dominican Republic, where fear of "another Cuba" has set the Johnson Administration on the course of aggression in naked disregard of all conventions of national sovereignty and international law.

superficial judgment would have suggested that Grivas black-mailed the British out of the island, rather than forced their withdrawal. So, in a sense, he did. But let us not be misled. The fact is that he and his handful of terrorists could not have done it without the active or passive support of the great majority of Cypriots. EOKA was an expression of the popular will, and, this being so, the British could have remained only by making war on the entire population. Since it did not suit their political and economic objectives to do so, they got out. So in Israel. So in Ireland.

Other examples are even more clear. Batista could not make war on the *fidelistas* without making war on the Cuban people. In the end, his resources proved inadequate to the task, and his regime collapsed.

The French, seeking to retain their interest in Indochina and again in Algeria, took arms against terrorists and found themselves, in both instances, fighting losing battles against a rising tide of popular insurrection. In theory, they might have subjugated Algeria (as they had done more than a century earlier) by spending more money, employing vastly more military manpower, and adopting sterner methods. But were these means really available to them in 1962? For reasons relating to the economy and internal situation of France and to the international situation as well, they were not. Even had the means and the will existed, it remains in question whether the game would have been worth the candle.

The last is the decisive question in all such contests between military power and popular insurrection in the modern era. It is the question that confronts the United States today, or will tomorrow.

The purpose of maintaining a colony is to exploit it, economically or for some political end. The purpose of supporting one political or economic system against another is to derive some benefit from it. The purpose of governing within a state is to enjoy the fruits of political authority, whatever they may be.

Yet in the modern era it is not possible to colonize or to govern profitably or to keep a subservient native government in power—in other words, to exploit—without the consent of the exploited. To kill them is self-defeating. To enslave them is, in the light of modern political and economic realities, impractical where it is not impossible. Hence the guaranteed success of any determined popular liberation movement once afoot.

This is the dilemma that will confront American policymakers wherever they come to grips with anti-American guerrilla movements.

In the United States of the last century, the government was able to crush the rebellious North American Indian tribes— because the Indians had no political or economic leverage. They were an inconsequential minority, alien in every way to the burgeoning white population, and what was wanted was their lands—not their labor, their trade, or their good will. Consequently, they could be exterminated wholesale at no appreciable cost. Indeed, it was economically and politically desirable that this be done—and it *was* done.

Conditions have changed in the world. What is wanted today is manpower and its products. The raw materials of the undeveloped areas are of no use to the industrial powers—the copper of Chile and the petroleum of Venezuela, for example, are of no use to the United States—without the human effort that makes them available; strategic bases require the services and the good will of large populations; industry requires both large labor pools and ever-expanding consumer markets.

Under such conditions, to try to suppress popular resistance movements by force is futile. If inadequate force is applied, the resistance grows. If the overwhelming force necessary to accomplish the task is applied, its object is destroyed. It is a case of shooting the horse because he refuses to pull the cart.

If such a destructive course is adopted, it can be only for one reason: to deny the object of contention, the disputed area, to a third party. This may prove to be the case in South Viet Nam, which has little value to the United States except *denial* value, as a great rice basket to be kept from the hungry Chinese.

The choices open to Washington in Viet Nam appear obvious. Unless the dissident Vietnamese population can be *persuaded* to embrace a solution acceptable to the United States (certainly a forlorn hope), the alternatives are: (1) to wage a relentless, full-scale war of subjugation against the Vietnamese people, with the aid of such Vietnamese allies as remain available; (2) seek a solution acceptable to the Vietnamese people, a step that would clearly entail negotiating with the Viet Cong; (3) quit the field and let the Vietnamese work out their own solution.

A fourth possibility does exist. Essentially it is a monstrous variation of the first. The United States can change the *character* of the war, or its apparent character, by expanding it; that is, by taking arms against Hanoi and, inevitably, against China. To do so, with the right kind of window dressing, could conceivably be justified in the minds of the American people and perhaps of their allies despite the tremendous expense and risk involved, where a losing war in the limited theater of South Viet Nam cannot be justifed. Under cover of a general war, the two Viet Nams could, perhaps, be occupied and put under martial law, and the Communist movement suppressed by overwhelmingly superior military force.

But then what? A Southeast Asia held by American troops in the overwhelming numbers that would be required (and it would have to be all of Southeast Asia, not merely Viet Nam) would be a burden almost beyond endurance for the American economy and the American electorate, and would be of no conceivable use under such conditions except as a base for the ensuing war against China. War to what end? It staggers the imagination to think of the vast, interminable, and profitless conflict that would ensue, even assuming that it were confined to Asia—and we have no such assurance. The bloody, costly Korean war would appear as a child's game by comparison.

\* \* \*

What of the future of guerrilla movements elsewhere?

In black Africa it seemed, not long ago, that the end of European colonialism and the emergence of the new republics could be the beginning of an era of peaceful progress. In fact, the demise of colonialism on most of the continent now appears to have been not the end, but rather the beginning of revolutionary struggle, having as its object the destruction of all alien, or at any rate all Western, interest and influence.

For the moment, a native army led by white mercenaries is able to defend Belgian and American mining interests in Katanga against a powerful if undisciplined insurgency. But the Congo is a vast jungle, big enough to swallow up a dozen South Viet Nams, and far more difficult to control. In the circumstances, it is hard to believe that a few hundred mercenary soldiers and a few dozen American warplanes can make any difference for long.

More troops, more guns, more money could prolong the struggle, but to what purpose? If the object were profitable exploitation of the natural and human resources of the area, then prolonged hostilities would be self-defeating: The cost would be greater than the stake. Yet a protracted war is precisely the kind of war the Congolese rebels are prepared to fight. It is, in fact, the only kind of war they are equipped to win.

If, on the other hand, the object were to deny the Communist bloc access to a strategic area, speaking in terms of Cold War objectives, then the questions would arise: For how long? And at what cost? And, finally, how many other such strategic arenas is the West prepared to defend? For clearly the Congo is not the only object of Cold War contention.

Many if not most of the new African nations remain within the Western orbit temporarily. That is to say, they are under the political and economic influence or control of their former colonial rulers, or of the Western, industrial bloc taken as a whole. Their governments are favorable, for the time being, to arrangements which permit the continued exploitation by the industrial West of their natural and human resources.

In other parts of the continent—Angola, Union of South Africa, Rhodesia—white, colonialist minorities still rule.

In all, without exception, it seems safe to say that revolution, spreading like a subterranean fire by means of guerrilla warfare, is not merely a possibility, but a virtual certainty, as the primitive black people who are the vast majority in Africa, emerging from tribalism and peonage, discover that they can be neither ruled nor exploited without their consent.

What applies to black Africa applies also to much of Asia and the Arab lands, and—of vastly greater importance to the United States—to almost all of Latin America.

The undeveloped countries that occupy three quarters of the globe—*under*developed is a euphemism—contain by far the bulk of the world's as yet unexploited natural resources, the raw materials of industry. Thus they are the prizes for which the industrialized quarter contends. Yet these same backward areas also contain the greater part of the world's population—the hungriest part, growing at a rate that far outstrips their rate of economic growth, needing, wanting, demanding more with every passing year.

How will that burgeoning population, growing hungrier and at the same time more aware day by day of the extent of the world's wealth, be kept under control once it has learned—and it is learning very rapidly—the lessons of guerrilla warfare? It cannot.

Colonial or native armies, even gendarmerie, could formerly do the job. The Cuban revolution has demonstrated that they can no longer do it, once a determined guerrilla movement is afoot. The mechanized armies of the industrial powers have no better chance, as Viet Nam and Algeria would seem to prove. For both terrain and the distribution of populations, as well as the nature of the struggle, determined by its objectives, favor the potential revolutionaries.

Tomorrow's guerrilla armies, in Africa, in Asia, in Latin America, will be drawn from the ranks of the world's *have-nots*, the hungry peasants and the urban slum dwellers who meet the first requirement of the guerrilla, having nothing to lose but their lives.

They will come from the productive labor force of the most exploited countries—and here the battle will be half won; for their labor cannot be obtained by killing them.

They will fight over the terrain that they know best and that most favors them, in the mountains and jungles and swamps where tanks and artillery and aircraft have least effect. And their natural camouflage and quartermaster and intelligence service will be the swarming population from which they spring, a population which cannot be destroyed save at the cost of destroying the economy and resources that are the prizes of the struggle.

How will the guerrillas be defeated when they are everywhere?

If technological superiority could defeat guerrillas, the war in South Viet Nam would have been over long ago. At this writing, the United States is spending—at the rate of nearly two million dollars daily—all the money it can usefully spend in the area. And the war is being lost. It is being lost to a poorly armed, numerically inferior enemy because mere technological wealth, translated into arms, aircraft, armor, military supplies, is not enough to defeat popular forces employing guerrilla tactics on their own familiar and friendly terrain.

The Pentagon could easily afford to commit ten or twenty times the number of aircraft and a hundred times the armor, artillery, rockets, napalm, and other weaponry presently being employed in South Viet Nam. It does not do so primarily because the targets for more weapons, more bombs, more napalm do not exist. Short of bombing South Viet Nam off the map, there is no employment for more bombs than the number now being used. Short of destroying all Vietnamese villages, there is no need for more napalm. Short of machine-gunning the Vietnamese peasantry *en masse*, there is no way to use more machine guns—because the Viet Cong against whom they might be used will not stand up and be shot.

To catch guerrillas requires overwhelming military manpower. For valid political reasons—the apathy and indifference of the nominally pro-Saigon Vietnamese, the American reluctance to commit substantial numbers of American troops—the manpower needed to hunt down and exterminate the Viet Cong simply has not been available.

\* \* \*

Yet South Viet Nam is, after all, a limited theater. Its area: about sixty-five thousand square miles. Its population: about sixteen millions. The conflict in South Viet Nam is, in the military jargon of the Pentagon, only a brush-fire war. To date, this single brush fire has cost the United States more than five and a half *billions* of dollars.

The question, then: What will the cost be when the brush fire becomes a forest fire, consuming all of Southeast Asia, flaring in Africa with its quarter of a billion people, spreading through Latin America with its restless, hungry, fast-breeding two hundred twenty millions?

Latin America, not Southeast Asia, is the area of prime concern for the United States, or should be. Potentially, it contains the explosive ingredients of a revolution that could radically affect the North American economy and the position of the United States among world powers within a few short years.

At the back door of the United States, stretching nearly six thousand miles from the Rio Grande to Tierra del Fuego, lies the battleground of tomorrow, a teeming continent of tangled jungle, trackless rainforest, towering mountain ranges, arid plains and swarming urban slums that contains all of the components—social, political, ideological, economic, and demographic—of violent revolution.

American arms cannot suppress insurrection in South Viet Nam, with its sixteen million people, then how will they prevail in, say, Brazil, with a population of seventy-five millions and a land area, half of it virtually uncharted tropical forest, of 3,286,270 square miles? The question is not rhetorical. Brazil has already come once to the brink of revolution, and is not alone among its neighbors in explosive potential.

If the United States cannot command the manpower to garrison Southeast Asia—and the outcries that arise in Congress with each fresh report of military casualties reveal the political impasse—how will it garrison the Andes, running four thousand miles down the South American continent? Yet this is what is in prospect, if the thinking applied to Southeast Asia is extended to an area much closer and far more vital to the United States.

In all of the twenty Latin American republics, from Mexico to Argentina,* varying only in degree, the same revolution-breed-

*Cuba excepted.

ing conditions exist—the same glaring discrepancies in the distribution of wealth, the same ghastly slums, the unemployment, the backwardness of the rural areas, the corruption of nominally democratic government, the surging birth rate outstripping the annual rate of economic growth, and in all, the same high popular anticipation of progress that is in itself the greatest single impetus to radical political action.

In Guatemala, Indians who speak little or no Spanish and live on the most primitive level of subsistence make up two thirds of the population. Feudal landowners, not least among them the United Fruit Company, control the commercial agriculture of this country, and an army led by a corps of officers of whom a third are colonels, the highest rank, puts down the student riots that break out from time to time in the capital, while the jails are filled with political prisoners. The U.S.-directed coup that overthrew the government of Jacobo Arbenz in 1954 canceled the modest social reforms that had been attempted by a politically leftist regime, but failed to provide a solution of social ills that continue to fester. Not surprisingly, a guerrilla movement has long been gathering strength in Guatemala.

In El Salvador, a few vast holdings, banana plantations and coffee *fincas*, occupy fully half of all cultivated land. Eighty percent of the farms are of fewer than twelve acres, and the two hundred thousand peasants who live on them scratch barely enough from the soil to stay alive.

In Ecuador, *per capita* income in 1959 was estimated at $160, but two thirds of the *families* earned $120 or less. In mineral-rich Chile, more than half of the rural population lives on a family income of between $100 and $135 annually, and in Brazil's chronically drought-ridden Northeast Territory, the annual *per capita* income is less than $75.

The monopoly of the arable land of Latin America by big estates is such that some 10 percent of the landowners own 90 percent of the land, stretching out in huge *latifundios* of thousands of acres, worked by laborers who live in shacks or barracks and are paid a pittance if they are paid at all, while the remaining 10 percent of the land is fragmented into tens of thousands of *minifundios* too small to provide the narrow margin of profit that would permit the purchase of fertilizer, of agricultural tools, or of any means of improvement.

Millions of rural Latin Americans live without buying or selling, on the fringes of a society in which they have no share or voice. Hundreds of thousands in the equatorial forests are the merest squatters, who burn off a patch of jungle, subsist on the meager root crop which it produces until the thin soil is exhausted, and then move on to burn another patch elsewhere, following a primitive pattern that was old when the *conquistadores* came to the New World.

Population pressures and starvation in the countryside drive hundreds of thousands of peasants to the cities to seek employment, and a new pattern of misery is formed. In Rio de Janeiro, the slums that line the hills ringing the city are called *favelas;* the waterless shacks of which they consist, one atop the other, house a quarter of a million Brazilians, inhabitants of a human jungle which even the police fear to enter. In Santiago de Chile, the slums that surround the capital are appropriately called *callampas,* meaning mushrooms; in Lima they are called, ironically, "the City of God"; in Caracas they are *ranchos*—all of these terms signifying the rat-plagued, disease-ridden, lawless shanty towns of a subculture in which millions of men, women, and children live without a foreseeable future, unless it is in the hope of revolution.

Poverty does not of itself engender revolution. But poverty side by side with progress creates a new amalgam; the hope of social change stimulated by even a little education produces a new social phenomenon: the ambitious poor, the rebellious poor, the cadres of the revolution, who have nothing to lose, and see much to gain around them.

Without a clearly articulated cause, without forceful and persuasive leaders, without political organization, generations of slum dwellers have lived and died in misery, generations of peasants have scratched the soil, and there have been few real revolutions.

What has changed in the twentieth century in Latin America?

First of all, the poor have become *poorer* and more numerous, and more desperate. There has been an unprecedented growth of population everywhere, a population explosion that has brought with it a corresponding *decline* in *per capita* income, in housing units, in the proportionate supply of the staples of common consumption, jobs, even water to drink. In Venezuela for example, the population increase in a single decade is estimated at more than one and a half millions, or 30 percent. In Brazil, the population rose from 52,000,000 to 66,000,000 in the decade between 1945 and 1955, and by 1963 had leaped to a fantastic 75,000,000 or more, for a gain of 44 percent in eighteen years. In the twenty Latin American republics taken together, the population rose from 163,000,000 to 206,000,000 in the years between 1951 and 1961, for an average annual gain of four millions; and the outlook is for a population of 265,000,000 (some say 273,000,000 would be a more realistic estimate) by 1970.

Meanwhile the rate of economic growth lags far behind. In 1960, the population rise was 2.8 percent, while the increase in over-all production was a negligible 0.3 percent and agricultural production *dropped* a full 2 percent.

Such figures speak for themselves. With every passing day, there are more hungry mouths to feed in Latin America and there is proportionately less food to feed them. And yet, strangely enough, their wants are not less, but greater than formerly.

For while the poor have been getting poorer, they have also become increasingly aware of the wealth around them, the *potential* in which they might share.

There has been, along with the population explosion, a revolution of communications, and out of it has come what has been aptly described as "the revolution of rising expectations." In Rio, a forest of television antennae rises over the *favelas:* The slum dwellers are bitterly poor, but not so poor as to lack the means to see the industrial progress and affluence that surrounds them, not so poor as to fail to understand that promises are being made to them, political programs invoked in their name—and to begin to stir with impatience for the day when the promises will be fulfilled. In the labor barracks of the Brazilian

Northeast, radio brings the message of the Cuban revolution, of fighting in Viet Nam and the Congo, of riots in Panama and Harlem. The plantation workers are poor, but not too poor to know what other men like themselves are doing, and how they are setting about it, and with what results.

Awareness creates, if not a revolutionary class, then a revolutionary base. Economic progress, however limited, is a revolutionary force in itself. Popular education, slowly spreading, stimulates emulation and social ambition. Commerce and industry, on however inadequate a scale, give rise to a certain social mobility. New political alignments are formed. New wealth, edging aside the old feudal elite, strives for political power. A middle class is created. Revolutionary leadership is found, first in the poorer and more ambitious or idealistic sectors of the middle class, then in the spreading new class of poor white-collar workers, who, scorned by both the middle class and the elites, unable to make common cause with them or to aspire to their privileges, follow the only avenue open to their ambition and form a radical political opposition, taking the cause of the humble and the disfranchised as their own.

Thus spreading misery creates a powerful revolutionary base, and progress provides it with incentives and leadership. Political organization follows. Its slogans, its selection of causes, are indicated by the social circumstances. Given the oppressive social and economic conditions of Latin America, it is not surprising to find that the ideological basis of most radical opposition movements there is at once Marxist, nationalistic, and stridently anti-Yankee.

The United States, with its great investment in Latin America, its control of vital industries—the price control which it exerts over the raw materials that the area sells and equally over the manufactured commodities that it must buy—and its history of intervention in Latin America politics, is obviously tailored for the villain's role.

As if this were not enough, Washington has openly declared itself the enemy of liberation movements in Latin America, since the Cuban revolution, by avowing its intention to intervene, militarily if necessary, to prevent any "Communist takeover" in the Hemisphere.*

Since the Latin Americans know very well that almost any change likely to be prejudicial to United States economic interests or political hegemony will be viewed as a "Communist takeover"—Communism, socialism, and anti-imperialism being more or less equivalent terms in the North American lexicon—it follows that war is already declared.

The first skirmishes have, in fact, begun. Sporadic guerrilla fighting has long been in progress in Venezuela, Guatemala, and Colombia; outbreaks have been reported in Bolivia, Chile, Peru, and Argentina; and certainly more will follow. Two million *peronista* ballots in the last Argentine presidential election can scarely be taken as votes of confidence in U.S. leadership or in the ambitious but slow-moving and inadequate Alliance for Progress, however good its intentions.

It would be an exaggeration to say that Latin America is, at this writing, on the brink of revolution. The *alianza para el progreso*, despite its faults, has had a palliative effect in some areas. Temporarily successful American intervention in Brazil has checked that country's drift to the Left. The Latin American Communists are deeply divided, as are the national Communist parties everywhere in the Western world. The old-line Communist parties in Latin America, which might have been expected to provide leadership to proletarian or peasant movements, are bogged down by their own conservatism, ineptitude, dogmatism, and opportunism; in many instances they have found an accommodation with the incumbent governments, and are content to do nothing and grow fat. The revolutionary following enjoyed, for a brief period, by the Latin American *fidelistas* has waned in proportion with the failure of the Cuban revolution to fulfill its first bright promise. Many who at first looked with favor on Fidel Castro, exhilarated by his defiance of the Yankee Colossus and sympathetic to the plight of beleaguered Cuba, have since been alienated by his alliance with Moscow and his involvement in Cold War politics—the missile crisis of October,

---

*A vow recently fulfilled in the Dominican Republic.

1962, being taken as the chilling object lesson of that involvement. The fate of the Cuban middle class, on an island grown gray and austere since the first heady triumphs of the revolution, has also been a disillusionment to middle-class Latin Americans.

The revolutionary base and the revolutionary ferment of Latin America nevertheless exist as potent realities. The seeds of popular insurrection have been sown broadcast. Its techniques are readily available to all. And although large-scale revolution may not be imminent, it seems safe to predict that within the next decade the United States is certain to face grave challenges to its leadership, its diversified economic interests, and perhaps even its security in the Western Hemisphere. Need one add: *and* in the rest of the undeveloped world?

Central America could become an American Viet Nam tomorrow. Brazil could become an American Congo. Venezuela, with its great petroleum wealth, an American Algeria. And the Andes, to quote Fidel Castro, a greater Sierra Maestra.

What is to stop it?

\*   \*   \*

Given the over-all backwardness of the area and the booming birth rate, economic plans on the order of the Alliance for Progress can only be palliative agents, not long-term cures. Land reform is the outstanding, obvious first step. Industrialization—impossible without markets, the elimination of illiteracy, and massive capital investment on an unprecedented scale—is the next.

But before these giants steps toward progress can even be considered, radical political changes must precede them. So long as the United States, in alliance with unrepresentative, oppressive, and corrupt governments, stands in defense of vested interests in Latin America, including its own great, exploitative investment, so long will the tap remain in the bottle and revolutionary pressures continue to build within—until the inevitable explosion.

True, dictatorial governments can be bolstered by military and economic aid. Cooperation can be obtained by bribes and economic coercion. Incipient guerrilla movements can be stamped out before they begin—the first, larval stage is, indeed, the only stage at which they *can* be stamped out. But, conditions remaining the same, others are certain to arise.

What is needed, then, is an entirely new, long-term approach to the problem of U.S.–Latin American relationships.

A logical beginning would be to abandon so-called military aid—the sop, granted in the name of hemispheric defense, to maintain the good will of military oligarchies whose only need of tanks and warplanes is to intimidate the people they nominally represent.

The next step—also logical but perhaps scarcely feasible in view of the domestic political realities of the United States—would be to declare an economic New Deal for Latin America: Such a New Deal would mean an end to the lopsided commercial relationships, the unilateral trade pacts, the economic extortion by means of which United States industrialists dominate Latin American markets and United States consumers fix the prices of the raw materials, the minerals and cash crops, on which the Latin Americans depend for their lives.

The third and most radical step, and the hardest, would be simply—to *embrace* the revolution.

Revolution cannot be suppressed. It may be channeled. Does it not make sense to seek to channel it in the least damaging, most hopeful direction?

Since in most Latin-American countries it is the middle classes and the growing class of white-collar proletariat rather than the workers or the landless peasantry that exercise revolutionary leadership, the chances are good that in many instances popular movements could be diverted into more or less bourgeois-liberal channels; in other words, that oligarchies and military dictatorships could be replaced by liberal democracies based on the limited socialism we mean when we refer to welfare government, and revolutionary pressures siphoned off by means of certain radical reforms, of which land reform would be the most obvious and immediate.

Failing such a solution, the choice would still remain between democratic socialism and its Marxist-Leninist alternatives. Nor does this exhaust the range of choice. On the radical Left still stand two or three main revolutionary groups: the old-line Communist parties, devoted to Moscow, and their Stalinist, pro-Peking offshoots; the more militant of the *fidelistas*, who also find an affinity for Peking; and the national socialists—using the label in its purest sense—who, while strongly influenced by the Cuban experiment, lean to a kind of American *titoism*, without Cold War commitments.

Looking back on the Cuban experience since 1958, one sees that the United States, at every stage, failed to pick up options superior to those that remained as the range of choice narrowed.

In 1957 and throughout 1958 Washington might have choked the Cuban revolution to death with cream by openly repudiating Batista and welcoming or actually assisting the democratic, then bourgeois-liberal, reformist movement led by Fidel Castro. To have done so would have been to strengthen the liberal nationalist elements that supported Castro and to have discredited the anti-Yankee extremists and especially the old-line Communists of the *Partido Socialista Popular*—at that time not at all popular with the 26th of July Movement.

A choice still existed through 1959 and well into 1960. It was too late to abort the revolution, and positive steps would have entailed the sacrifice of considerable immediate U.S. dollar interest: The Cuban land reform inaugurated by the *fidelistas* was a crying necessity as well as a pledge that could not have been ignored. But Washington would have been wiser to subsidize it than to fight it. Further expropriations of American poverty might and probably would have followed. At its worst, however, the loss related to the socialization of the Cuban economy would have been only a limited dollar loss, and much of value might have been retained: a market for U.S. products then ranked as the sixth largest in the world; important commercial and banking relations; an assured, unfluctuating sugar supply; above all, an amicable if independent Caribbean neighbor instead of a hostile Cold War base.

To embark, instead, on a campaign of diplomatic and economic strangulation was not merely to cut Cuba adrift, but to drive her in the only direction in which she could go: toward utter dependence on the Soviet Union. It makes no difference to argue that Castro and his followers may have wished, or even *did* wish, to go there. The fact is that it could have been prevented. Every geographical and economic consideration leads to that inevitable conclusion.

Tomorrow, or next year, or the year after that, similar choices will present themselves—they are already indicated—in one or more of the countries of the Hemisphere that North Americans still consider to be theirs. The revolution certainly will not stop with one country or a few. The entire undeveloped "third world" is in transition, and it is all moving in the same direction, under the multiple pressures of economic and social and political necessity.

The United States can make the accommodation that it *must* make with the forces of revolution. Or it can, in the end, be destroyed. To take the course of accommodation will not be merely to acquiesce to the inevitable, but to declare a partnership with it. That means:

¶ To declare diplomatic and economic war on the Latin American oligarchies as we have declared war on Cuba, and to break with those governments strong enough to resist or retaliate.

¶ To actively assist revolutionary groups—expediently selected—with arms and funds and advisers, acting on the premise that if our present military aid program for military dictatorships, our "advisers" in South Viet Nam, our weapons air drops in the Escambray of our Bay of Pigs invasion can be sanctioned under international law or morally justified in violation of it, better and more expedient causes can be even better justified.

¶ To openly proclaim the United States a champion of revolution so as to steal the thunder of Moscow and Peking and to offer the emerging third world a viable alternative to Marxist-Leninist totalitarianism on the one hand, and Western imperialism, "styled Free World leadership," on the other.

The expedient course might, even at this late date, apply to Cuba. If aid to Tito, then why not aid to Castro? There is a contradiction here that needs to be sorted out. Tito never had atomic missile bases, true. But then, never having been invaded, he seems never to have felt the need.

It may be that Castro can safely be left to stew in his own juice. Cuba isolated is Cuba disarmed—perhaps. But Latin America is not Cuba; it is a continent larger and more populous than our own, and cannot long be left to ferment without producing a great stench and devastating explosions.

To stand against revolution in the Western Hemisphere will be to embark on a profitless and interminable war that cannot be won. It will be to choose rioting, strikes, sabotage, bloody insurrections, and political and economic chaos on an unprecedented scale, culminating inevitably in a series of grueling and protracted guerrilla campaigns from Mexico to Argentina, involving more and yet more American troops in endless offensives without objectives, battles without victories, sacrifice without compensation, and, ultimately, defeat at a cost too fearfully high to be even remotely reckoned.

To compromise with revolution may well be to surrender the greater part of some twenty billions of dollars of vested interest in Latin America: That is indeed the outlook. It will mean, besides, to sacrifice much of the economic advantage of the lopsided trade treaties and coolie labor on which a substantial part of our prosperity is based.

On the other hand, the prospective loss *could* be considered as another sort of investment. Great as the immediate dollar loss would be, it would merely match the twenty billions that have already been earmarked for the Alliance for Progress. And the long-term dividends would be far greater than any amount of dollars. They would consist, first of all, of continued, certain access to the vast supplies of vital raw materials on which United States industry is absolutely dependent. Continued trade, on a more equitable basis, would be guaranteed, and with it the promise of expanding markets for American manufactured products and agricultural produce, based upon the rising wages and consumption of millions freed from peonage and brought into the twentieth century. And finally there would be the element of security which seems to preoccupy our policymakers. It is inconceivable that the United States can wish to live in a divided Hemisphere, half of it hostile to us; yet the only security to be obtained in this respect must be based on genuine hemispheric co-prosperity, and that in turn it must inescapably be based on the social justice which will be the battle cry of the gathering Latin American revolution.

On the one hand, progress, prosperity, and security; on the other, certain disaster. There is only one outcome to guerrilla war, and that is revolution, and there is only one remedy, and that is peace. Some will call it surrender. If so, it is the surrender of force to reason, based on the understanding that no people can be subdued or kept in subjugation who do not accept defeat.

# INDEX

ROBERT TABER traveled to Cuba in the late 1950s as a CBS investigative journalist to cover the country's burgeoning revolutionary movement. He became an eyewitness to history as he marched from the Sierra Maestra to Havana with the ragtag revolutionaries, led by Fidel Castro and Che Guevara, who forced Batista to flee the country. Taber also wrote *M-26: Biography of a Revolution.*

Foreword author BARD O'NEILL is professor of international affairs at the National War College, Washington, D.C., where he is also director of Middle East studies and director of studies of insurgency and revolution. O'Neill has written or edited several books including *The Energy Crisis and U.S. Foreign Policy, Armed Struggle in Palestine, Insurgency in the Modern World*, and *Insurgency and Terrorism.* He and his family live in Springfield, Virginia.

)